The fastest way to write your book

The fastest way to write your book

Dave Haslett

ideas4writers

First published in Great Britain 2005

ISBN 0-9550116-0-4

Published by
ideas4writers
PO Box 49
Cullompton
Devon
EX15 1WX

Printed and bound in Great Britain
By Antony Rowe Limited, Eastbourne

For Kate

Contents

1   Introduction

Welcome to *The Fastest Way To Write Your Book*. Here's the plan: we're aiming to spend one week coming up with The Big Idea, researching it, planning the book and creating an outline. We'll then spend three weeks writing the first draft. That's zero to finished first draft in under a month. Not bad, eh? We'll still have to edit it and polish it of course, so allow another week or two for that. And then we have to sell it – as quickly as possible. That, in a nutshell, is what this book is all about.

You'll need to undertake a certain amount of preparatory work. That doesn't mean preparing the book in advance; it means preparing yourself. You might need to learn a new skill, such as touch-typing, or improve an existing skill, such as learning to type faster.

This book will guide you through over two hundred techniques that will allow you to write a book in the fastest possible time. The process won't necessarily be an easy one, but it will be fun, and the potential rewards are enormous. Imagine writing ten bestselling books in a year. Or twenty in two years.

You certainly won't need to use all the techniques in this book. Around twenty should be enough if you choose the right ones. Somewhere in this book is the perfect combination of techniques for you. It's up to you to decide what they are, then study them, master them, and put them into practice.

This book is for:
- Those who would like (or need) to write a book but can't seem to find the time.
- Writers who want (or need) to build up a large body of work very quickly.
- Writers who don't want to spend several hours a day slaving over a word processor.

This book won't teach you *how* to write. There are plenty of good writing tutorials and courses available. You'll find details of some of these in the Resources section. And if you'd rather let your story develop slowly and find it's own way while you write at a leisurely pace then this book is also not for you.

Back in the mid 1980s, I wrote two novels. They weren't very good, and the three publishers I sent them to rejected them. Each book took nine months to write. Since then I've started and abandoned two more – and learnt how to write. The first draft of my fifth novel is just about finished. It needs an extensive rewrite but I don't have time to do it. The whole thing is sitting in my head getting in the way of other thoughts. I need to get it written and out of my system.

The idea of starting ideas4writers.co.uk was that I could run the website in only one or two weeks per month, leaving the rest of the time free for writing. It didn't work out that way of course. ideas4writers.co.uk is in constant development and I still don't have any free time for writing. But at least I now get to choose my own working hours.

Meanwhile, not only is this fifth novel cluttering up my brain, but I've had a great idea for a sixth one too – and a seventh and eighth. But novel number six is topical – I need to get it written and published before a certain forthcoming event happens.

It was obvious that if I wanted to write books *and* run ideas4writers.co.uk *and* still have a life then I needed to find some other way of doing it.

I'd already read about people who had written their books quickly. According to *The Guinness Book of Records*, Barbara Cartland wrote twenty-six books in 1983 – that's one every two weeks. And according to the *Encyclopaedia Britannica* she wrote a staggering 723 books in her entire career. Ray Bradbury freely admits that he completed the first draft of *Fahrenheit 451* in nine and a half days. According to Terence Blacker in his book *Kill Your Darlings*, Jack Kerouac wrote *The Subterraneans* in three days. George Simenon allowed himself six days to write a *Maigret* novel. Walter Scott finished two *Waverley* novels in three weeks. Ernest Hemingway, D.H. Lawrence and Evelyn Waugh all completed a novel in six weeks. These examples prove it can be done. I've mentioned other examples later in the book.

Then there's National Novel Writing Month (NaNoWriMo), which takes place each November. The aim is to write a 50,000-word novel in thirty days. That sounds great, but most entrants just abandon their lives for the month and "write like hell". Only fifteen percent of entrants actually finish their novel by the deadline. The other issue I have with NaNoWriMo is that the organisers freely admit writing this way is "stupid" and the result will be "crap". According to them, "aiming low is the best way to succeed". I disagree in the strongest possible way. If I'm going to spend thirty valuable days writing my novel then I expect it to be as good as I could possibly write, regardless of the timescale. I'd also want my novel to be a full-length one – 80,000 words or more – not a 50,000 mini-novel that would be virtually impossible to sell. I'm obviously going to need a better strategy than "writing like hell" and "aiming low".

Even more extreme is Canada's three-day novel writing contest, but that's just plain crazy. I can't offer you any help there except "write like hell". Or don't do it.

A poke around the internet revealed several websites offering courses and manuals telling you how you – yes, you! – could write a book in fourteen days or twenty-one days or twenty-eight days. All would be revealed in return for an enormous fee. Further research revealed that most of these were scams.

That made me even more determined to find the secret – or secrets. I'd already discovered some of the basic techniques while researching ideas for ideas4writers.co.uk. All I needed to do was to put all the pieces together – and come up with a lot more ideas. Then I wanted to actually write a book using these techniques to prove to myself that it worked.

Well, I'm delighted to tell you that it *does* work. This book took just twenty-three days from initial idea to completed first draft. And I managed to achieve all that without making any changes to my lifestyle.

I'm certain that if I can do this then so can you. So I offer you this book, which serves as proof that the methods within it really work. I hope it brings you great success – please let me know if it does.

By the way, if you want to enter the next NaNoWriMo do bear in mind that you'll have an unfair advantage over the other entrants.

2   Why write a book and why write it fast?

Why write a book?

There are so many reasons that it's hard to know where to start. Let me list three personal reasons.

Firstly, I'm a writer and I need to write. When I'm not writing I'm not truly happy and the ideas clutter up my head. The urge to write nags away at me.

Secondly, the ideas keep on coming. The longer I spend not writing, the more ideas I have for more things to write about and the more the urge to write grows. It's useful to have ideas4writers.co.uk as an outlet for some of these ideas, but I like to keep some back for myself.

Thirdly, I want to be remembered when I'm gone. I want to leave a lasting legacy. Most people live ordinary lives and when they die they're forgotten. What a waste. I don't want that happening to me. I want the world to remember me and value the contribution I made. What better legacy than a good book?

Those are my reasons for wanting to write books. Let's consider some others.

Sometimes people expect you to be a writer even if you don't consider yourself one. You might be a speaker, training instructor, teacher or coach. When people regard you as an expert they'll ask you for more information to take away with them. They trust you to supply them with this information – and they know you have it. Not only do they want you to be a writer; they expect it. The important point is that you're not starting from scratch. You already have the information; you just have to write it down.

Once you've written a book, your credibility skyrockets. You stand out from the crowd. You'll be in more demand as a speaker or teacher or coach. You'll be able to charge more for your services and people will willingly pay it, because your book *proves* you're an expert. They'll buy your book even if it covers the same material that you've already taught them. Of course, it's a great selling point if your book contains much more information than your speech or training session. Mention that during your talk and your sales will increase.

What about your ego and personal pride? Writing a book is more than most people ever achieve. Many people start writing one but never finish it. Can they really call themselves writers? Maybe. Maybe not. They aren't sure. They might call themselves writers but have a nagging doubt. But if you've not only started writing a book but *finished* it, then you truly can call yourself a writer.

There's the fame thing to consider as well of course. Do you want to be famous? If so, do you want to be famous as a writer? Or do you want your fame as a writer to lead to fame in another field? If you've written a bestselling book you can be as famous as you want to be. Join the media circus and appear on talk shows, book-signing tours, radio phone-ins, quiz panels and much more. Or shun publicity, stay at home, and write the next book.

Then there's recognition. This might be recognition within your company, within your industry, or by the public – which is the same thing as fame. If you write a book about the industry you work in, think what a career booster it could be. You might scoff and say your boss wouldn't think much of your book and it would do nothing for your career. That may be true. But there are other companies and other bosses. Add your book to your CV or résumé and apply for another job. It'll put you well above the other applicants. If you choose to stay with your current employer, you'll find your colleagues now treat you with more respect even if your boss doesn't. Writing jobs will come your way when they need to draft a new advertisement, or a brochure, or a business plan, or an article for the company magazine. Your writing talent has been recognised!

Do you have something important to say? A book lets you disseminate that message to a wide audience. Your message might be one of entertainment if you're a storyteller. Or it might be a message of hope or peace or love. Perhaps it's a warning, telling people their future is at stake unless they act now. Maybe you've found a new technique that will enrich people's lives or help them improve their circumstances. Perhaps you've come across vital new information. Don't just tell a few friends; write a book and tell the world. If it's a powerful message it'll get out eventually anyway and someone else will write the book – and make a lot of money out of it. You'll curse yourself for not having done it when you had the chance.

Are you happy with your job? Do you like sitting in traffic every morning and evening? Do you like waking up at some unearthly hour to the sound of an alarm clock? Are you happy with just four or five weeks' holiday each year? Are you happy arranging your life to fit in with your company's demands rather than your own needs? Life doesn't have to be like that. As a professional writer you can live wherever you like, work whatever hours you like, take time off whenever you want, avoid traffic jams and throw the alarm clock in the bin. How does that sound to you? Luxury? Maybe. But you could do it. You don't even have to be a full-time writer to make major changes to your life. If you could make enough money from writing to cover half your salary, you could work part-time and give up working mornings. If you're a morning person, you could give up working afternoons and go to the beach or the golf course instead. Or you could downsize from your stressful City career and take a more enjoyable job nearer home.

How secure is your job anyway? No one wants to think about redundancy or enforced retirement, but if you work for someone else there's always a chance it could happen. As a writer, you're never without a job. If you need more money, write another book or increase your marketing effort on an existing one.

Writing books is also a great way of making money – if you can do it. Not everyone can of course. Some slave away for years and never make a penny. One advantage of this book is that you'll discover you don't have to slave away for years to find out that you aren't a good enough writer - you'll know within a month or two.

When you work for an employer, there's a limit to how much you can earn. There's your salary, overtime and (possibly) bonuses, but that's it. Lack of money severely cramps your lifestyle and your freedom. By writing books, you can work harder for greater rewards. The more you work, the more you earn. Your income can go beyond your salary and perhaps replace it entirely. Some people become seriously rich by writing books. That could be you. You either have to write one or two exceptional books or lots of good ones. I'll show you how to take the latter approach, but that doesn't rule out the possibility that some of your books might also turn out to be exceptional.

There are hundreds more reasons for wanting to write books, but I'll end this section with one last one – and it's a good one. People want and need books. They need entertainment. They need education and information. Bookshops need products to sell. We like to curl up in bed with a good book. Books keep us company when we're feeling lonely or bored or ill. We use books to relax and unwind; we take them on holiday with us. Books improve our lives and increase our knowledge. Books let us find out about ourselves and the world we live in. People love books. Someone has to write them. Shouldn't it be you?

Why write it fast?

You could certainly spend two years or more writing your book if you really want to. But if you have a busy life it's hard enough finding any time to write at all. Spending two years on a single book would be an impossible luxury.

Just because you're producing a book quickly doesn't mean there has to be any reduction in quality. If you write in your own voice, the words you end up with should be the same no matter how long it takes to write. The time factor is therefore irrelevant. By following the methods in this book, you should be able to write twenty books in two years rather than just one. And each book's content will be identical to one that would have taken the full two years to write the old way.

Let's assume you've written your book in a month. You don't have to tell people you wrote it that quickly. Most people believe it takes at least a year to write a book. And the longer it takes, the better it must be. So tell them it took two years. When they see the quality, they'll believe you. Although you might have to write them under several different names so they don't get suspicious!

Another advantage of writing a book quickly is that you don't have time to get bored. Writing at high speed is exciting! Many writers abandon their books simply because they've become bored with them. That doesn't mean the book itself was boring. It means the writer was unable to maintain an intense interest in the subject or characters for such an extended period. It probably seemed quite an exciting project at first. The book might have an excellent structure and the writing might be of the highest quality. If they could only finish it, it would do well. But they got bored. After two years that's not surprising. When you write a book in a month there's no time to get bored. It's one big adrenalin rush and lots of fun – especially when you see the finished product growing before your eyes. It's even more fun when you know you can sell the result.

By all means spend two years writing your book if that's what you really want to do. Take the time to play with sentence construction. Spend a week finding *le mot juste*. Spend an entire morning adding a single comma and the entire afternoon taking it out again. However, I suggest that you spend the first two years writing several books the way I describe in this book. Then you can live off the earnings and spend as much time as you like on your magnum opus. (Although you'll probably be having so much fun by then that you'll churn out the magnum opus in a month too.)

Here's another reason why writing quickly is a good idea: freedom. The money you make from writing means you can spend less time at work and more time doing what you enjoy. Do you feel guilty about not spending enough time with your children or grandchildren or friends? Why not spend a month writing your book and then enjoy yourself for twenty-three months? You'll still produce a book every two years. You don't even need to give up your spare time for that one month. I'll show you how to write your book in odd moments and lunch breaks, and perhaps an hour or two at the beginning or end of the day. You'll be able to complete your book within a month without sacrificing any of the quality time you spend with your family and friends.

Two months from now you could be holding a finished book in your hands, even if you haven't started writing it yet and even if you have no idea what it'll be about. You can start selling it immediately. As you finish other books, you can sell them too. By the end of the first two years, you could have twenty books on sale. If each of them sells as well as the one single book you'd normally have written in that time then you've generated twenty times as much income. If one or two don't sell quite as well as expected, so what? Others will probably sell better than you expected. Consider the life of an average writer, turning out a single book every year or two and making a steady living from it. There's absolutely nothing wrong with that. Except that to produce twenty books might take him his entire working life. You could produce the same number of books in just two years. I'll leave you to decide what a difference that could make to your life.

3   Before you start

Let's look at some general hints and tips to help you start writing your book faster. There's no magic here, just common sense. The magic comes later. But you need to have the basics in place first.

Ergonomics
It's important that your computer, desk and chair are set up properly and that you're comfortable. Make sure you know how to do this – the staff at your local computer shop will be able to advise you. Also make sure your screen is clean and free from glare.

Getting organised
Another thing you can do to make your writing life easier – and faster – is to have all your reference materials and research notes to hand so you don't have to stop writing to find them.

Just write
One of the big secrets of writing quickly is to just write. Don't stop to look anything up while you're writing. If you know the subject well enough then the answer is in your head anyway. If you don't know the answer, make it up or leave a gap. You can fill in the correct details at the editing stage. It's also a good idea to keep a notepad handy so you can leave yourself notes about the bits that will need fixing.

Aural distractions
Are you distracted by noise? Does absolute silence kill your inspiration? A solution to both problems is to have music playing in the background. It gets rid of the silence, blocks out noise, and provides a rhythm for you to type to. The interesting thing is that within a few minutes you'll no longer hear the music. Your mind is concentrating on your writing and 'forgets' the music is there. It comes as a shock when the music ends. You're brought back to the real world with a jolt. Surely it can't be finished already? Since you don't really

hear the music, it doesn't make much difference what you play. It doesn't have to be gentle; pop and rock works just fine.

On the other hand, some people can't bear music playing when they write. If that's you, you could try natural sound recordings. There are plenty available: flowing streams and rivers, waves, thunderstorms, country meadows, forests and jungles, birdsong, whale noises, and many more. You can also get recordings of natural sounds mixed with panpipes, flutes or guitars.

Time of day

Are you a morning person or a night person? You might think that it doesn't matter, but in fact morning people have an advantage when it comes to writing. And if you're a night person, you might think the best time for writing is after everyone else has gone to bed. Not so. You're tired. You've had a long hard day. Your energy is low and your brain is winding down. It's actually better to skip the late night writing session and go to sleep early. Get up in the morning before everyone else and have your writing session then. Your mind is refreshed and your body is gearing up for the day ahead, so you'll actually gain energy as you write rather than lose it. Give it a try for a couple of weeks and you should notice a significant improvement in your productivity.

Having said that, I have to confess that I'm very much a night person myself. I've tried doing early mornings and it kills me.

Sleep

Sleep is important to writers. You're far more productive after a good night's sleep. The ideas come easily, you feel more positive about your writing ability, and more optimistic about your chances of success. Dreams are important too, but I'll discuss those later in the book.

Exercise before writing

If you're planning a long writing session, how about getting a bit of exercise before you start? Clear your mind with a brisk walk or ten minutes on an exercise bike. Or how about some yoga or gentle stretching? Anything that gets your body warmed up and the blood pumping to your brain is good, otherwise you'll slump in your chair, feel tired before you even start, and the writing will be difficult.

Try exercising at the end of a long writing session too. Your muscles will have seized up and you might have built up quite a bit of tension or frustration that needs to be released. Try some more stretching, perhaps followed by something more vigorous later in the day.

Dancing along to happy music can also cheer you up. (If that sounds too embarrassing, do it when you're alone and can't be seen.)

Take a break

Sometimes you really do need a break from all that writing. If you've spent the entire morning writing, don't go into the afternoon session for an hour or so. Do something that gets you away from the physical act of writing. It's even better if it also allows you some thinking time. You can still be writing in your head while you're away from your desk. What you can get up to depends on your personal circumstances, but here are a few suggestions. Go for a bike ride, swim lengths at your local pool (but don't count how many you do), go to the gym, go for a walk in the country, have a long walk or jog along the beach, or walk the dog. While you're doing whatever it is, think about what you're writing and any problems you're having with it. Let the solutions – and further ideas – come when they're ready.

Writers write well

One vital skill all writers need is the ability to write well. That doesn't necessarily mean being literate and physically writing or typing your work – you can get someone else to do that for you. It simply means being able to communicate your knowledge or story well. You can hold an audience spellbound, or fill them with excitement about your subject, as well as filling them with knowledge.

If you can't write well then any time you spend writing is wasted. You need to have confidence in your ability. Take a writing course. Find out where your weaknesses are and get them sorted out now, rather than wasting time writing something that's fundamentally flawed.

It really is worth taking the time to do this. You'll make up any lost time very quickly once you've mastered the basic techniques. You should then be able to sell just about everything you write, rather than hoping to get lucky – or hoping no one notices how bad you are at dialogue, characterisation or punctuation.

Read as many books on the craft of writing as possible, and do all the exercises in them. It takes years to learn to play the piano to professional standard. How long have you spent learning the craft of writing? Be honest.

The more I practise, the luckier I get

Another secret of writing success is simply to get on with it. The more you write, the more likely it is that inspiration will hit you – usually while you're writing. And if you write regularly, you're going to complete some pieces of work. That's more than many people ever do – including some who claim to be writers. Reaching the peak of achievement requires daily practice (and loving it). This is more fully explored in the book *Mastery* by George Leonard.

Know your subject

If you're writing non-fiction, you need to know your subject inside out before you start writing – or at least those aspects that you're going to write about. The more familiar you are with the subject, the less research you'll have to do and the quicker it will be to write the book. Practise explaining things to people. Try explaining an aspect of the subject to someone who knows nothing about it. Then ask him if he understood it. If he claims he did, ask him to explain it back to you. If he has problems, consider how you could rewrite that section to make it easier to understand.

If you're writing fiction, you need to be a great storyteller. Never miss an opportunity to spin a good yarn. You don't have to make it up on the spot – try out some of the material from your new book and see how well it goes down with an audience. Then see if you can improve it. If you walk into a room and people urge you to tell one of your stories, you're well on the way to success. On the other hand, if they try to avoid you then you still have some way to go. That's an easy test of your writing skills.

Write using your speaking voice

The easiest way to write quickly is to aim for a conversational style, just as you speak naturally. Use your own voice, as if you were telling the story (or explaining the subject) to a friend. Be yourself. Don't be over-formal or pompous. Be a wise friend and an entertaining guide, not a smart-alec know-it-all.

A passion for writing

You need to be passionate about your writing. And not only must you be passionate, you must communicate that passion to your readers. If you're excited about your work, you can't get bored with it. You'll write more quickly, and with enthusiasm and excitement.

Before you start

Before you even start writing your book, try to come up with the following things:

- A great title.
- The table of contents – list all your headings and sub-headings.
- An outline.
- A one-minute marketing blurb.
- A brief profile of your target audience.
- An introduction – why you're writing this book and why you're the best person to write it.
- A marketing summary for the back cover.
- An irresistible query letter to an agent or editor.

Use these things to guide you as you write; they'll help keep your mind focused on what you're trying to achieve. We'll look at each of these in more detail later in the book.

Visualise the end product

As you prepare the outline, and later when you're actually writing the book, try to keep in mind what you want the end result to look like. Can you see your finished book in your head? Imagine holding it in your hands and flipping through the pages. Imagine a reader picking it up in a bookshop, flipping through the pages, reading the back cover. See his eyes light up; it's exactly what he's looking for. He takes it to the checkout with a smile on his face, then races home to read it. He might even send you a letter when he's finished, telling you how much it meant to him.

As you write, always think of your readers. Put yourself in their position as you plan the book they really want and need. Answer every question they could possibly ask, and many more besides. Fill them with enthusiasm about the subject. Tell them where to get all the extra information they'll need if they want to take the subject further. Tell them the best places to buy equipment. Entertain them. Write the best book you're capable of writing. Pack it with as much information as you can squeeze in, or as much action and excitement as you can invent. You owe it to your readers and to yourself. It'll make the writing easier. It'll make getting published easier. And you'll feel happier about yourself, knowing that you produced a first-rate book rather than a third-rate one.

Think it – write it

The best technique for writing your book in the fastest possible time is to create the whole thing in your head before you start writing it. When you start writing, the book will then come together as fast as you can write or type it. So you need two things: a detailed outline and the ability to write or type quickly. We'll look at both of these in later chapters.

You need a deadline

You need a target to aim for. In this case it's easy: your target is to come up with the Big Idea, refine it and research it, prepare an outline, and write the first draft – all within a month. We'll look at targets and deadlines in more detail in Chapter 16.

Targets and timescales

How you choose to divide up the writing stage is really a matter of choice. Some people like to set themselves a daily target – number of words, number of pages, number of chapters. I prefer to let the book set its own timescale. At the end of each day I record how much I've written, but I don't have a daily target.

Progress chart

Some people like to chart their progress on a graph. This is an interesting thing to do, and it's very motivating to see your graph growing as the days pass. I don't bother with them myself, but if you think they'll help then give them a try. I find that when you're writing at this sort of speed, seeing your book coming together in no time at all is motivating enough.

Books that write themselves

I know you're itching for me to start revealing secrets so you can get on with some writing. Don't worry, there's plenty of that to come in later chapters. But here's a little something to whet your appetite. Some books really can write themselves. Simply come up with a good angle for a book, then contact your local newspaper to tell them about your plans. See if they're interested in doing a story about you and your project. If they aren't interested, you could always take out a small advertisement in the newspaper. Invite people to send in their stories, histories, ideas, successes, failures, or whatever it is you're writing about. Most people will gladly share their experiences and be delighted to have their words appear in print. (And they'll buy your book and tell their friends about it.) All you have to do is choose the best contributions, group them together, and edit them as necessary. You might want to write a brief introduction to the book and a few sentences to introduce each section, but that shouldn't take long. And that's it done – the book's finished. Remember to let the newspaper know, because they'll probably want to do another feature on you – which is free advertising for your book of course!

Editing can wait

Don't even think about doing any editing until the entire first draft of your book is finished. Characters, for example, have a habit of going their own way, so you might have to rewrite earlier chapters. You won't know this until the very end of the book. There's no point editing chapters as you write them, or you'll end up editing every-thing twice. Anyway, you don't want to interrupt the flow of your writing once you've started. Editing makes you highly critical of your work. That's a good thing when you're editing, but it kills your creativity. Keep writing until the very end of the book. Never go back over what you've written and start polishing or changing it. That's what most people do. And it's the single most common reason why most books are left unfinished.

Ideally, you should stop work after the first draft and get on with something else for at least three weeks. Why not write the complete first draft of your next book? Then you can come back and start editing your work with a fresh eye. I'll take a closer look at the editing process in Chapter 18 and give you lots of techniques to speed up the process. Remember, we don't want the editing to take more than a week or two.

Print as you go

Something I always do at the end of each day is to print out whatever I've written. You'll need to work from a printed copy when it comes to editing, and it makes sense to print it out as you go in case something happens to your electronic copies.

I take my newly printed pages and put them in a box file. (If you're writing longhand, tear out all the pages you've written that day and put them in the file.) I label each page with the chapter number, name of the topic or scene, and the page number. This makes things much easier when it comes to editing. In fact as soon as I've completed my outline, I make a summary page for each chapter and put that in the box file too. If I come up with any ideas that I could include in chapters I haven't written yet, I then have something to attach them to and they won't get lost. This is important. Ideas are very easy to lose. And to lose a great idea is an incredible waste.

Laptops and portables

I like to be able to work on my book wherever I am, and I don't like having to sit at my desk to write. So I have two portable computers which I can take with me wherever I go – or use while lying on the bed or curled up on the sofa. I'll tell you more about these in Chapter 13.

Always keep a back up

Finally in this chapter, I'd like to show you the method I use to manage and back up books on my computer. I use a PC running Microsoft Windows, but if you use a different sort of computer you should still be able to follow the process quite easily.

In *My Documents* I create a new folder with the title of the book or a word or two to identify it. I then divide the book into chapters, create a new document for each chapter, and save them in the folder I just created. I name the files *chap01.doc*, *chap02.doc*, and so on. Using leading zeros makes sure they get displayed in the right order, otherwise the computer thinks *chap2.doc* comes after *chap11.doc*.

Close the folder, then right-click on it and select 'Send To...' and then 'Desktop as shortcut'.

The folder now appears on your desktop, which is a handy place to keep it as you'll be using it regularly. Note that this is just a shortcut, not the actual folder. If you delete the shortcut, the real folder will still be in the My Documents folder.

Double-click the folder on your desktop to open it. If you double-click on any of the chapter files within it, they should open up in your word processor ready for you to work on.

> Microsoft Word will automatically save a copy of your work every few minutes if you turn on the Autosave feature. Click on the Tools menu and choose Options. Go to the Save page and tick the box labelled 'Save AutoRecover info every xx minutes'. I've set mine to ten minutes. If the program crashes or the power fails, Word will 'autorecover' your document next time you run it.

That's how I manage a new book, but how about backing it up? You'll often hear tales of woe from professional writers who've lost all their files or had their laptops stolen. Replacing a laptop is fairly simple. Rewriting your entire book isn't. Always keep a back-up copy. And don't forget those printouts I mentioned earlier.

At the end of the writing session, close down your word processor, insert a floppy disk, then look in the folder on your desktop and find the file you've just been working on. Right-click on it and choose 'Send to' then '3.5" Floppy (A:)'. That gives you your back-up copy. Remember to send a copy of the file you've been working on to the floppy disk every time you finish working on it.

You should be able to get all the chapter files for your book onto a single floppy disk. If the book is very large, save the first few chapters on one disk and the rest on another. Alternatively, you could do what I do and use CDs. Most computers now have built-in CD writers and the back-up process is much the same as saving to floppy disk.

> If you use Microsoft Word, turn off the option to 'Allow fast saves' otherwise your files will become enormous. That's because Word saves every change you make. The more changes you make, the bigger your files will become. With the fast save option turned off, your files will only contain the current text.

Ideally, you should have at least two sets of back-up disks and give one to someone else to look after. That way you'll still have a copy of your book whatever happens.

To password protect a document in Microsoft Word, click the Tools menu, choose Options, then click on the Save tab. Enter a password in the 'Password to open' box, then click OK. You'll be asked to enter the password again to confirm it.

One other backup solution worth mentioning is the free web space your Internet Service Provider (ISP) gives you. Most people don't realise that this can also be used for other purposes. You usually get at least 10 Mb of free off-site storage space, which is enough for several books. Password protect your documents, then upload them to your web space. You'll need to check your ISP's instructions on how to do this. Because the files are password protected, nobody else will be able to open them. But if disaster ever strikes you can easily retrieve them using any computer with an internet connection

You might be wondering what to do with all those separate chapter files once your book is finished. There are four options:

1. Leave them as they are but set the page numbers in Chapter 2 onwards to start at the correct number, rather than 1.

2. Copy each file and paste it into a single large document that contains the entire book. This can be useful if you want to add a table of contents or an index.

3. Use your word processor's Master Document feature, which allows you to treat the book as either one large document or as separate chapters. I don't use this feature myself as I find it unwieldy and not particularly reliable.

4. Import the individual chapter files into a desktop publishing program and assemble them into a book there. This is the best option if you're self-publishing your book.

The next step
In the next chapter we'll look at the fastest ways to find great ideas.

4 The fastest ways to find great ideas

If you're going to be writing a book every month or so, you're going to need plenty of ideas. So let's head straight for the idea mines and start digging for gold . . .

Ideas find you
The first thing to bear in mind is that ideas seek writers out; you can't stop them. It's important to be ready for them though, because ideas don't hang around for long. As soon as an idea flashes into your mind, write it down there and then. Don't wait even for a few seconds or it will be gone.

Write them down immediately
It's a good idea to carry a notepad (and a pen or pencil of course) around with you – or do as I do and use a handheld computer. Keep some paper and a pen next to your bed too. I get some of my best ideas just as I'm drifting off, and I can't get to sleep until I've written them down.

You can get small diaries with little pencils that slip into the spine – ideal for keeping in your pocket. I've also seen tiny notebooks that clip onto a key ring. You always have your keys with you, so you'll always have a notebook too. Keep a small cassette recorder or digital voice recorder in your car.

You can use a mobile phone for recording ideas if you've nothing else to hand. Write yourself text messages – you don't have to actually send them. Store them in the outbox and write them down when you get home. You could also phone home and leave a message, or phone a friend. You have no excuses for missing a great idea.

A child's view
Look at what's happening around you. What if you didn't understand it? How could you make sense of it? A child who has never seen smoke coming out of a chimney before might think the house is on fire.

He might become distressed and want to rescue the people inside – terrific story potential. What other aspects of life might a child misunderstand? Spend some time talking to children and find out what they think about various things. If you don't know any children of the right age, go along to your local primary school and offer to talk to the children about writing books, help them with their reading, and help them to put together their own stories.

Art

Art galleries make excellent sources of ideas. Have a look at the paintings of street scenes for example. What's going on in the background? What are the buildings like? Could you set your story there? What are the people doing? What do you imagine them getting up to? What made the artist want to paint this particular scene? Is the artist famous? Did he have an interesting life? How did the painting come to be in this gallery? Did the gallery buy it from the artist? Is it for sale? Did it once belong to someone else? If so, what happened to him? Why isn't it still in his family? Is it cursed? Is it worth a lot of money? Might someone want to steal it? Which paintings in the gallery are the most valuable? If someone wanted to steal one, how would they do it? What security systems are there?

There are many other sources of paintings. Art books, for example, can be found in libraries, bookshops and second-hand bookshops. You can also get CD-Roms featuring the great artists, paintings and galleries. You'll also find plenty of art collections, photographs, and other images on the internet.

Biographies

When you read biographies, look out for references to minor characters: crazy brothers, humorous shopkeepers, and mad uncles, and the tricks and stunts they pull. A good biography can produce a rich crop of interesting characters and amusing tales. You can also combine the events in the biography with elements from your own life to produce an interesting combination. Try selecting an interesting-looking character who was in the background at some major event. Describe what happened from his point of view. He'll have plenty of other things going on in own his life of course. And he might have made considerable sacrifices or overcome great adversity so he could attend the event. How will this have changed him? What sort of life is he going back to?

Books

When you need ideas on a particular subject, nothing beats a good book. Try skimming the headings and thinking about every topic or concept you come across. If that doesn't give you what you want, read it again more slowly. You might come across a single item that triggers a whole load of ideas. You could also search the internet for articles on your chosen subject.

Childhood

Even in a very ordinary childhood, many things will have happened by the time you reach the age of fifteen or sixteen. Family members have come and gone, friendships have been made and broken, relationships have begun and ended. Then there are all the adventures you had during the school holidays, made-up games with bizarre rules, toys, pets, the school bully, lessons, teachers, sports, and much more.

Classified adverts

You'll sometimes see some very strange things for sale in your local newspaper. How did they ever get hold of one those things? Why did they want one in the first place? Why are they getting rid of it? Even the more mundane items could have interesting stories behind them. What if you see several items for sale at the same address? Could that be a woman selling her husband's belongings because he ran off with someone else? Is someone selling his possessions to cover a debt? What if the possessions don't actually belong to him? Does the real owner know he's selling them? What if the real owner tries to buy something from him?

Curiosities

Sometimes, if you look around properly, you'll see the strangest things. They might not make complete stories, but they do make interesting curiosities you can use to liven up dull descriptions. Things that seem out of place are worth taking a closer look at. For example, I know of a country road where there's a gas cylinder propped against a wire fence. What's that doing there? Perhaps the farmer wanted an electric fence but he had to make do with a gas one until he gets mains electricity installed. (I know you can use a battery, but use your imagination.) Perhaps someone put it there as a joke. Maybe it fell off a lorry. What other reasons can you think of?

Daydreams

Daydreaming is one of the best ways of getting ideas. Look around you, read something, look at a picture, or whatever you want. Now close your eyes and picture what you've just seen. Let your mind wander around the scene: in it, through it, beyond it. What thoughts does it trigger? What does it remind you of? What's happening outside the scene? Are there any interesting stories, characters or settings you could make use of?

Try thinking of somewhere you'd really like to be – a deserted beach, a tree house in the middle of a forest, or a country meadow. Imagine that you're there, relaxed and happy. Now let your mind wander and see what happens.

Dreams

Dreams can lead to all sorts of great ideas. That's why it's particularly important to have writing materials next to your bed. Write down your dreams as soon as you wake up. You might have dreamt about something that would make an interesting character, plot twist, or scene in a novel. After you've been writing down your dreams for a while, look back over all the dreams you had in the last month, six months, or year. Do you see any patterns? Could you link separate dreams together to create a story?

Dreams can be useful for non-fiction writers too. Many scientists and inventors have said that their greatest ideas and breakthroughs came to them in dreams.

Things aren't always what they seem in dreams, so a book that analyses their meanings makes a useful addition to any writer's bookshelf. It'll also give you something interesting to browse through when you need inspiration.

Try discussing your dreams with a friend and see if you can come up with your own meanings. It doesn't matter how accurate or absurd they are. The important thing is that you're generating great ideas.

You could also try drawing pictures of your dreams rather than writing a description. It doesn't matter if you can't draw – nobody else needs to see them. Use plenty of colour and make your drawings really vivid. Drawings help you to remember much more about the dream than words alone. You'll also get many more ideas from a drawing of a dream than from a description of it – a really vivid drawing could inspire hundreds of different stories.

Apparently we all have several dreams every night, although we often can't remember anything about them. According to sleep researchers we have our first dream about ninety minutes after we go to sleep, and we spend more time dreaming at the end of the night than at the beginning. Here's something you could try: set an alarm clock to wake you up a couple of hours before you normally get up. (Put it under your pillow to avoid disturbing anyone else.) If you were dreaming when the alarm goes off, write down what it was about. If you weren't dreaming, go back to sleep and try again the next night. If it doesn't seem to be working, try setting the alarm to go off a little earlier or later until you find a time that works for you. Don't wake yourself up more than once a night. Once a week will be enough for some people.

Eating certain foods just before you go to sleep can also encourage dreaming. Things that are hard to digest, such as cheese, are known to encourage dreaming. Bread and rice can also work well as they soak up fluids and make you thirsty. When this becomes too uncomfortable, you wake up desperate for a drink. When this happens to me I often find I've just had a very weird dream indeed. But remember what I said earlier about ideas disappearing. Write the dream down first, and then have a drink.

The thirst system is less predictable than the alarm clock system, but the results are usually stranger and potentially more useful – it depends what sort of writing you do.

Drawing and doodling

Try thinking about a problem or idea with a pen or pencil in your hand. Write down the main words and draw lines to link them together. Add more words and lines and see where they lead. Add little drawings, doodles and diagrams to explain how things connect together, or draw anything that comes to mind. Doodling lets your subconscious communicate directly with the outside world. You should find that the solution to your problem comes much sooner than if you just tried thinking about it. You'll also generate considerably more ideas.

Gossip

Gossip can make an excellent basis for stories, plots and subplots, as well as characters and dialogue, so start collecting it as soon as possible. Ask your friends to listen out for gossip and to phone you as soon as they hear anything juicy. At the very least, they should write down what they heard so they can tell you about it next time they see you. People love to listen to gossip – and this gives them the perfect excuse. And the more friends you have collecting gossip for you, the more ideas you'll have.

Guidebooks

If you want to include a particular location in your book, try to find a guidebook that tells you all about it. These often include surprising facts about places you thought you knew well. The author will usually live locally and might even be a member of the local writing group, so if you need more information you should be able to contact him quite easily. Guidebooks usually include details about the history of the place, so you could include real events and famous (or infamous) characters from the past in your story – or at least refer to them to add interest.

Guided tours

Most towns and cities have guided tours. These are definitely worth going on, even if you've lived there all your life. The guides will probably take you to places you've never seen before, and tell you about the unusual histories of buildings you pass every day. Many guides are also excellent storytellers and tell intriguing tales about local characters, villains, misdoings, ghosts and legends.

Have a good look at the factories and industrial buildings near where you live. Some of these will undoubtedly be worth a visit and they might even give guided tours. If they don't have official tours, ask if someone could show you around. Tell them you're a writer and most will happily oblige.

Who knows what you might discover. They might use chemicals that would make very effective poisons, for example. And do they have any machinery that could maim its operators? You'll hear some real horror stories about these!

The buildings themselves are likely to make interesting locations for your story. You could also consider writing a book about the company, or a history of that particular industry.

Horoscopes

Look at several different horoscopes for a particular day. Do they all agree? Probably not. That could give you several ideas. You could also use someone's horoscope to decide the outcome of an event in your story. Perhaps someone's taking an exam and you can't decide whether he should pass or fail. His horoscope says his mind is elsewhere that day, so you decide to make him fail the exam. Problem solved.

Perhaps you're halfway through a story and you run out of ideas. What should your character do next? Read several different horoscopes and see if you can find anything interesting for him to get involved in.

ideas4writers.co.uk

The ideas and inspiration website for all writers – and undoubtedly the fastest way to find great ideas. ideas4writers.co.uk has a massive online database containing thousands of ideas in over thirty categories. Whether you write fiction or non-fiction you'll find tons of ideas here. Most ideas also come with useful examples to show you how you can use them in your own work. You'll also find lots of little-known tricks and techniques to help you get published, sell more books, and come up with ideas of your own.

Non-fiction writers will love the lists of historic anniversaries – given months in advance so you have plenty of time to write about them. Fiction writers will love the writing engines – mini computer programs that automatically generate characters and storylines with just a click or two of your mouse.

You can chat to other writers in the discussion forums and send in samples of your work for feedback and advice. And there's always an expert on hand to answer your writing, computing and word processing questions.

I don't have room to describe it all here, so why not try it for yourself? At the back of this book you'll find a voucher for three months' free membership, worth £7.50.

Job shadowing

While you're taking a guided tour around business premises (see above), ask if you could spend a day with someone who works there. He'll just carry on with his job as normal, but you'll tag along too and watch what happens. You'll also have a chance to ask questions and make plenty of notes. This is a great way of getting to know what the job is really about, and learning the procedures, equipment, and technical terms properly. You can then include these in your story to give it a ring of authenticity. You'll also get the personal perspective of the person doing the job. What's it *really* like? What strange experiences has he had? How did he get this job? What made him apply for it? Did he always want to do this job? Is it anything like he expected it to be? What other jobs has he done? What qualifications does he have? What training did he undergo? Would he rather be doing something else?

Kicking-out time

You'll find a terrific source of ideas towards the end of an evening when the pubs are near to closing. Pick a lively one and go in for a drink or two. Then hang around in the background and watch and listen as trouble starts to brew. Some people will have had quite a few drinks. Their inhibitions have disappeared and they're ready to tell their so-called friends exactly what they think of them. This can be a goldmine of ideas if you don't mind experiencing the sharper edge of life.

Librarians

If you need ideas and information on a particular subject, ask your local librarians for help. Get to know them. Make friends with them. They're nice people – and they aren't just there to check books in and out. Reference librarians can be especially useful as they keep all sorts of interesting books in their storerooms.

Look for ideas

Do you constantly look for ideas? Whether you write fiction or non-fiction, short stories, novels, magazine articles, or poetry, ideas are all around you. If you think constantly about writing, and keep reminding yourself that you're looking for ideas, then you're far more likely to spot them. If you go about your daily business without actively looking for ideas then you're going to miss quite a few good ones. And don't forget your notepad.

Look for the unusual. You might not find something every single day, but you should see something intriguing at least once or twice a month. When you spot it, make a note, then think about the story behind it. What could this thing be? Is it in an unusual location, or is someone using it in an unusual way? Is it a strange design, invention or fashion? If you stay at home waiting for ideas to come to you, you'll miss this sort of thing.

Memorable events

Think about what happened yesterday, or a week ago, or a month ago, or a year ago. If something has stayed in your mind that long then there must be something interesting and memorable about it. So maybe it deserves a place in your book.

Newspapers

If you read newspapers thoroughly you'll discover that each page is bursting with ideas, stories and background material you can use. Look at the smaller items – the single-paragraph stories, fillers, and quirky human-interest pieces – rather than the main features. Professional writers can get a book commissioned by simply picking up the phone to their editor and reading out a newspaper article. The good news is that they'll be too busy plotting their new novel, screen-play or self-help guide to bother with the mass of ideas to be found a few pages further on in the same newspaper.

It's a good idea to clip out every item that interests you and keep it in a file. Mark each clipping with the date and the name of the paper it came from. Browse through these occasionally, looking for inspiration.

Many newspapers now publish internet editions. Sometimes you have to pay to access their archives, but the current edition is usually free. It's worth checking a number of these each day as you search for ideas – add each newspaper's website to your Favourites list. You can also find useful articles in online newspapers from other regions and other countries.

It's also worth having a closer look at the sections in your local paper that you don't usually read. The jobs pages, business news, church news, planning applications, legal notices, sports pages, family announcements, wedding photos, advertisements, and so on. Could you use any of these in your book?

How about reading some newspapers and magazines that you don't usually bother with? These can be a great source of ideas and background information for such things as clothing and fashion, homes and gardens, careers and lifestyles, personal problems and solutions, and so on. Specialist magazines will give you the authentic technical information and jargon words you need. You don't have to understand it, but you must use the correct terminology – and get someone else to check it.

If you find a particularly interesting article, you could research the subject in more depth and write a book about it.

When visiting somewhere for the first time, always make a point of buying a local newspaper (or read it for free in the library).

Old folks

Members of the older generation often have amazing stories to tell – if only people would let them. But nobody wants to listen to them rambling on, so their adventures go unrecorded. Talk to your older relatives and ask them about their lives, particularly their more unusual experiences. Go to a hospital or old people's home and befriend someone who never gets any visitors. As he learns to trust you, he might share secrets he's carried with him all his life and never told anyone else. If you come across a great story, make sure you ask for his permission to use it.

Opposites

When you've come up with an idea, try thinking about the exact opposite. For example, you might decide to write about a shiny new sports car. List its opposite properties: old, slow, broken down, rusty and so on. Think about what might cause it to get in such a state: an accident, a breakdown, theft, neglect, fire, and so on. Did someone tamper with it? Did the owner die and leave it to someone who didn't care for it? How about if someone finds a sports car rotting in a barn and he believes that a famous racing driver once drove it? Perhaps he could restore it to its original condition, if only he could persuade the current owner to sell it to him . . . and find enough spare parts . . . and prove that it really is the famous car and not a fake . . .

Other uses

Think about the other uses an object might have. Consider a tree, for example. It could be:

- A home for birds and squirrels.
- A climbing frame or swing for children.
- Wood for a timber merchant.
- Raw materials for a paper merchant.
- A hiding place.
- Fuel for a fire or stove.
- Shelter from the rain.
- Shelter from lions, tigers or bears who are chasing you.
- Food for some animals.
- Food and income for a fruit farmer.
- A job for a tree surgeon.
- A meeting place or a landmark.
- Medicine, in the case of certain trees.
- Material for a beaver's dam.
- A sacred object.
- Inspiration for an artist.

Look at the objects around you. What else could someone use them for, other than their 'proper' purpose? Try making a list. Use your imagination. By the time you've finished you'll probably be buzzing with mental energy and have come up with several ideas for things to write about. Can you see any connections between the items on your list? Do those connections trigger any ideas for stories, characters or events?

Overheard conversation

Sometimes you can't believe what you're hearing. You might catch the end of a discussion and hear something completely out of context. The most mundane discussion about, let's say washing powder, can easily turn into an amazing story about three little old ladies involved in a drug-smuggling ring. It helps if you have a lively mind.

And then there are the people who get things slightly wrong. They tell a story but make mistakes, or they sing along to a song and get some of the words wrong, usually with hilarious results. Listen out for these mistakes and see if they spark any ideas in your mind – once you've stopped laughing.

People watching

This is one of the best – and fastest – ways of finding new characters. Sit in a café, railway station, or anywhere busy and make notes about the people you see. You'll see people carrying strange objects. You'll see people in a mad rush, panicking, too busy to be polite, pushing others aside. You'll have no trouble spotting great characters for your next story – and getting a few plot ideas along the way too.

It shouldn't take long to compile a terrific cast of characters. Since this is such a quick and easy way of finding characters, spend a few more minutes concentrating on different aspects of people's personalities. Characters have 'character'. They aren't just short or tall, thin or fat, young or old, beautiful or ugly. Look for people who stand out; these often make the best characters. Look at the way they walk, talk, argue, approach someone they know, approach someone they don't know, greet someone they haven't seen for a while, say goodbye to someone they're fond of, and so on. Have a think about what they might be doing there, where they're going, who they're meeting, who they might be running away from, what jobs they do, what their hobbies are, and so on.

Here's an interesting exercise. Go up to several people and ask them all exactly the same question. You'll need a question that requires them to think of an answer, rather than giving a simple "yes", "no", or "quarter past two". Watch how they react as they think about their answer. Do they give an answer immediately? Or do they scratch themselves in various places, look around for clues, panic, or stare at you blankly? Do they walk away without answering? When they finally give an answer, how do they say it? Are they confident, hesitant, nervous, or friendly? Was their answer correct? Or did they just make something up to get rid of you? What sort of accent do they have? What does this say about them, their backgrounds, their jobs and habits and so on?

This exercise only takes a few minutes, but you'll come across people with all sorts of peculiar quirks who'll make fantastic characters for your stories.

Photographs

Dig out your old photographs and have a good look at the things in the background that you might not have noticed before. Perhaps someone strayed into the shot. Perhaps there's an event going on, or people going about their business. Does anything catch your eye? Look for things that take you by surprise, then think about how you could make a story out of it. Why was the photo taken? What if the people in the background were committing a crime? What if someone was convicted for that crime, but this photo proves he didn't do it?

Pre-owned belongings

Have a poke around a junk shop and see what curiosities you can find. Look for strange or interesting items and those that show some history. Hold each item in your hands and examine it closely. What is it? What was it used for? What else might it have been used for? Who might it have belonged to? How did he get it? What happened to him? How did it end up here? Look for signs of damage. How might that have happened? Has the damage affected its value? You could also try searching charity shops, jumble sales, car boot sales, antique stalls, and so on.

Problem pages and true-life articles

You'll find these in women's magazines and those aimed at teenagers, and they're always a good place for ideas. You might read about a failed relationship, abuse, a child who went missing years ago and then turned up again, and all sorts of other things. You can turn these stories into novels, or explore them in more depth in non-fiction books. You could also include a collection of similar cases in a non-fiction book, together with strategies for overcoming the problem.

As you read some of these articles, you'll learn about the areas of life that people have the most difficulty with. Look at the advice given. Do you think it would work? Can you see a story developing out of this problem and the reply?

How about an agony aunt who deliberately gives misleading advice? Why on earth would she do that? Is someone paying her? Or blackmailing her? How about a roving agony aunt who fills in when the regular aunts are on holiday?

Quotations and proverbs

Writing contests often use these as a starting point for a story. You needn't restrict yourself to entering contests though. Find a book of quotations, proverbs or phrases and pick out a few that catch your eye. What stories does each one suggest? What characters come to mind?

Running and jogging

Not only is this good for you, but you get a terrific sense of pounding rhythm as you run. Your mind wanders, and ideas start to come. Remember to carry something with you to help you remember those ideas. Don't just hope that you'll remember them. You might remember one or two, but the rest will be forgotten – what a waste of effort.

Slips of the tongue

We all make a slip of the tongue now and again. There's no need to get embarrassed about it. It's entirely natural and shows how passionate you are about what you're saying. And it's a great source of ideas. Whenever you make a mistake (or when someone else does) write it down as soon as possible. It's great fun to look through your collection from time to time. What do they suggest to you? Story ideas? Interesting characters? Witty dialogue? Short scenes?

Talk shows

TV shows such as Oprah, Jerry Springer, Ricki Lake, and Trisha can produce hundreds of great ideas very quickly. They form a massive source of human interest stories, problems overcome, personal tragedies, secrets and lies, and so on. These stories are about real people, so you could write to the show and ask for contact details for the people featured. Or use the people and their stories as a starting point for your own characters and plots. If a story particularly grabs your attention, you might like to research it further and write a book to help others who find themselves in a similar position.

Television

Look at each of the main terrestrial TV channels in turn, spending no more than a second or so on each one. Make a note of what image is being shown, and if you can tell what's going on make a note of that too. Once you've got all four (or five) images, try to make some sort of connection between them. Here's what happened when I tried it. BBC1: anti-war protesters wearing skull masks ride bicycles through London. BBC2: an extreme close-up of a black man singing while the credits scroll up over his face. ITV1: frozen meat defrosting because bad weather caused a power cut. C4: teenagers tell ghost stories in a haunted house where they're spending the night for a bet. There are some great ideas for a story there, and all for no effort whatsoever. Give it a try.

The invisible writer

Imagine you're invisible. You can go anywhere and do anything, yet not be seen. Where will you go? What goes on behind closed doors? What do people get up to when they think they're alone and nobody is listening? Here's your chance to find out. If your neighbours are having an argument, you could slip in unnoticed and listen. Why are they arguing? Maybe you suspect a gang of crooks is planning something. You could easily listen in and find out what they're up to. But what would you do with that information? You couldn't tell the police the truth about how you got the information, so what would you say instead? Perhaps you could have a go at stopping the crooks yourself. What other super-human skills might you have, and what might you be able to find out as a result? You could even write a story about someone (perhaps even a writer) who has super-human skills.

Typing and spelling mistakes

I'm thinking mainly of your own mistakes here, rather than other people's. Typing errors are more likely to happen when you're writing fast of course, but that's not necessarily a bad thing. You'll find some interesting ideas when you come to edit what you've written. Whenever you need to make a correction, pause for a second and consider the possibilities. You'll sometimes come up with bizarre ideas that you'd never have thought of otherwise.

Most word processors have spell checkers these days, and that can lead to interesting results too – especially when they try to correct people's names.

Unique-ness

If you're writing about trees, for example, look at every tree you come across. What makes that tree unique? If you had to find the same tree again, how could you be sure it was the same one? Think about how it looks, and how you could describe it vividly, or in a new way, so everyone would see that tree in the same way you do.

Walking

Go for a long walk by yourself in the country or along the beach, carrying a pocket tape recorder with you. Find somewhere quiet and secluded so you can think freely without distractions and interruptions and speak into your tape recorder without embarrassment.

I find it takes twenty or thirty minutes before the first ideas start to come, but by around fifty minutes or so they're generally arriving in floods. By the end of a long walk, I usually have a whole tape full of usable ideas.

It's all to do with finding the right frame of mind. Once you're tuned in, the ideas come as fast as you can speak them into the recorder. You need to be completely relaxed. Forget about everything else, and don't worry about whether you'll get any ideas. This isn't a good technique to use when you're up against a tight deadline – although the walk itself should do you some good.

Weird things happen

Ask people about the strangest, weirdest, most bizarre things they've ever seen or had happen to them. Ask everyone: your friends, your family, your doctor, your dentist, or the person sitting next to you.

The world is a stranger place than you can possibly imagine. The people you talk to are your witnesses, and most of them will be delighted to tell you about it. If you can't find a way of using these strange events in a story, why not make them into a non-fiction collection? You could start by writing a newspaper or magazine article that includes a few examples, and then invite readers to send in their own examples. You could then put the best submissions into a book – which saves you having to write it.

Wishes

Make a list of all the things you wish were true. For example: money grew on trees, cars could fly, children had volume controls, and so on. Once you get started you'll find it hard to stop. Now think of all the stories you could write where these things actually happen.

Worst-case scenario

If you're writing a story and don't know what happens next, here's a simple way to proceed: think about the worst thing that could possibly happen at that point. Don't just pick the first thing that comes into your head. Make a list of at least ten possibilities, then pick the best one, or the most intriguing one, or the one that would cause the greatest setback, or the one that's closest to the story's theme, or the one that logically connects with something that happened earlier in the story. (If nothing happened earlier in the story, go back and plant something.)

Write something

I often find that once I start to write about something, new ideas form with very little effort. As I write, I have ideas about better ways of saying things, additional items to include, different directions to consider, ideas for follow-up books, articles, stories, and so on. Each idea builds on what I've already written. Unfortunately, if you haven't actually written anything there's nothing to build upon. Thinking about writing will only get you so far. To be a real writer you need to write. I hope that doesn't come as too much of a shock!

Yellow Pages

If you're completely stuck for ideas, grab a copy of the *Yellow Pages* and pick three entries at random. What connection might there be between these companies? Could there be a criminal connection? Could the same person or family own them – maybe brothers or cousins? Perhaps they're all part of a larger parent company, or they've been the subject of a take-over bid. Are they run by a bunch of cowboys? Are they legitimate companies, or part of a scam? Could they be a front for a criminal or terrorist organisation involved in drug smuggling, money laundering, or arms trading? Perhaps they aren't real companies at all, but fake ones set up by a TV reporter who wants to test how gullible people are. Perhaps they're run by vicious rivals who use outrageous marketing tactics to steal each other's customers. What other tricks do they get up to? There's plenty of scope here for crime stories, legal or business thrillers, comedies, or even romances.

Your job

No matter how mundane your job is, you must have had a few 'odd' days. Try to recall the strangest, funniest, or most embarrassing things that have happened. If you can't think of anything, ask your friends about their jobs. One person's recollections will soon spark off someone else's memories of an even more bizarre incident. They'll come up with fantastic examples of odd behaviour involving managers and customers, funny incidents, the delivery driver who forgot about the low bridge, the customer who wouldn't leave, and many more. Include some of these incidents in your stories – or make up some of your own.

Your life

Wherever you live, whatever you've done, whatever your job and circumstances, your particular combination of life experiences is unique. Make a list of all the things you've done, the places you've been, the jobs you have had, and the things you can do. Is there anything there that you could write about? How about a non-fiction book about your hobby, or an unusual problem you overcame?

***

Never dismiss an idea

Most people have plenty of ideas, but they think of them as 'silly thoughts' or games that their minds play. They have a little smile to themselves then forget them. Perhaps they'll tell someone else one of their 'funny stories', but do nothing more with it. A *real* writer records every one of these 'silly thoughts' and tries to find ways of using as many of them as possible. Most will need refining to create something usable, and some will never be used, but that's perfectly natural. Many more people could become writers if they stopped thinking of themselves as 'someone who has silly thoughts' and thought of themselves as 'someone who has ideas'.

Let your idea mature

Having found your great idea you might be tempted to start writing immediately. Don't. Write your idea down if you haven't already done so. Maybe add a few additional notes. Then leave it alone for a while. You need to give your idea time to mature. This might take a few days; often it takes much longer. You'll know when it's time to move on to the next stage – planning, outlining and writing – because your brain will tell you to get on and write it, and you feel guilty if you don't. By then, the whole thing should have formed in your head, so getting it down on paper should be relatively easy.

The next stage

By now, you should have some sort of starting point for your book. All you need is a rough idea at this stage, even if it's just a single word. In the next chapter we'll look at techniques such as brainstorming and mind maps. These will help you to expand your idea, discover how much you already know about the subject, and find out how much research you'll need to do.

5   What you already know

Now that you've found your idea, let's see how much you already know about it and try to expand it into enough material to fill a book.

Start by narrowing your topic

Is your idea or subject too big for one book? If you've chosen to write about history, for example, that's too big a subject for a single book to cover. You'll need to choose a specific period in history. Even that might be too large for one book though, so you'll need to narrow it down even further. Perhaps your book could cover the differences between rich families and poor families of that period, or international trade, transport, education, or health.

Narrowing your subject like this will also speed up the research process. In fact, you probably already have a reasonable knowledge of the subject. It's all in your head somewhere, and the more you can retrieve at this stage, the less you'll have to research later – and the sooner you can get writing.

With that in mind, here are some techniques to help you find out what you already know.

Freewriting

The only tools you'll need for this technique are pen and paper and an alarm clock. You could use your word processor if you prefer, but switch off the screen so you can't see what you're typing. Set the alarm to go off in one hour, then let your mind relax. Spend one minute concentrating on your book's subject or theme and letting your thoughts flow freely. Then start writing and don't stop until the hour is up.

Start by listing the main topics or key events. Then fill in the details. Write about absolutely anything that comes to mind. Don't stop to correct any mistakes, and don't delete anything if you change your mind and decide it's no good.

You might like to imagine you're sitting an exam. You have just one hour to remember everything you know about the subject and to put it into some sort of order, with a proper beginning, middle and end. However, if you go to pieces under such pressure, just relax and list the thoughts that come to mind. Don't worry about the time or the structure.

What makes freewriting work so well is that you never stop writing for a single moment. Once you've got properly started you'll realise you know far more about the subject than you realised. There's no way you could possibly get it all down in one hour. Jot down all the main points and leave yourself notes about other details and areas that you can explore in more depth later on. Write quickly. Try to capture everything.

If your mind goes blank, it doesn't mean you've run out of information, it's simply that your mind can't get to it. Keep writing the last word you wrote over and over again. Your conscious mind will soon get bored and hand over to your subconscious, which knows exactly what you need. It retrieves loads of new information from your brain, and off you go again.

When the hour is up, stop writing and review what you've written. I'm sure you'll be impressed. You now have the beginnings of your book. It's probably a jumbled up mess right now, but we'll sort that out later.

Brainstorming

Brainstorming, like freewriting, is all about letting your mind run free. Think about your idea or subject, then write down every single thought that occurs to you, but this time in the form of a list or set of bullet points. Don't reject or correct anything, even if it sounds stupid or wrong. Those silly ideas might inspire other ideas that aren't so silly. In fact, you'll probably find that some of your best ideas are inspired by those you nearly rejected.

You're aiming to produce a long list of random thoughts, ideas, facts, memories, phrases, notes, jokes, song lyrics, images, dreams, people, doodles, books, magazine titles, and so on. As you think of one thing it should inspire something else. Add that to the list too, even if it doesn't seem relevant.

A brainstorming session can be as long as you like, from five minutes to two hours. The duration depends on you, the subject matter, and the amount of time available. If you haven't tried brain-storming before, try a twenty-minute session and see how you get on. Some people recommend a one-hour session, but I think that's too long if you've never tried it before.

Don't stick to the clock too rigidly though. If the session is going well and the ideas are coming thick and fast, keep going for goodness sake. Similarly, if the ideas dry up before the end of the session then call a halt. Don't sit staring blankly at the page. If the ideas run out, you haven't necessarily reached the limit of your knowledge. You've simply reached the limit of what your brain is prepared to retrieve during this particular session. Have a break and then try one of the other techniques in this chapter. Even if you think you've failed, you might already have enough information to start planning your book. We'll look at the fastest ways to fill the gaps in your knowledge in the next chapter.

With your list complete, most how-to books would now recommend that you leave your list alone for a few days so you'll be able to evaluate it with a fresh eye. That's all very well in theory, but we haven't got time. So, if you held your brainstorming session in the morning, take a leisurely lunch and do the critical review in the afternoon. If your session was in the afternoon or evening, have a good night's sleep and return to it in the morning.

The critical review

Now you can start being critical. Read through the whole list before you start considering whether to accept or delete items. Do some of the items fit together? Can you see connections between them? If so, draw lines to connect them or circle them to show they belong together.

Now you can go through the whole list, one item at a time, deciding whether to keep or reject each item. You might like to score each item against a set of criteria: relevance, decency, interest, plausibility, feasibility, and so on. If you decide to reject an item, think back to the brainstorming session and see if you can remember the thought process behind it. If you still think it's a stupid idea, cross it out.

When you've deleted the rubbish, you should be left with a list of your core knowledge about the subject, and perhaps you'll have a vague idea of how the book might look. You might also start to think about the gaps in your knowledge, and how little you know about the topics. Fortunately, research is one of the most enjoyable parts of writing a book.

Key word review

Another way of carrying out the critical review is to go through your list underlining all the key words. These will become the chapters and major sub-headings or plot lines in your book.

There are some other brainstorming techniques, so let's look at those too.

Mini brainstorm

For a non-fiction book, you need to list everything you can think of about the subject and ensure the whole subject is covered. You can get this list by going through the chapter titles and sub-headings in other books. Use several books if you can, to ensure that every possible aspect is covered.

Now hold a mini brainstorming session where you consider each item on your list and try to explain it in your own words, or break it down into the topics you want to cover in your book. If you can't think of anything, or you don't know anything about it, leave it and move on to the next one.

You should come to one of five conclusions about each item:

(a) You know a great deal about it, so writing about it will be easy.
(b) You know something about it, but there are a few gaps that need researching.
(c) You know little or nothing about it, so you'll need to do major research or leave it out.
(d) What you know about it seems to be the opposite of what everyone else says, so you'll need to double-check the facts.
(e) It's irrelevant as far as your book is concerned.

Brainstorming your reader

Consider who you're writing the book for. Make a list of your typical reader's characteristics: their background and lifestyle, how much they already know, why they want to learn more, what they expect to gain from your book, and so on.

Question brainstorming

In this technique, you try to come up with as many questions as possible that you could ask about the subject or idea, rather than looking for answers or trying to list everything you know. After a suitable break, go through your list and decide which questions are good and which are useless. As before though, don't delete any question without pausing for a moment to see if it inspires anything else. When you're happy with your list of remaining questions, go off and find the answers.

Question brainstorming is a relatively new technique that's rapidly gaining favour. The best thing about it is that a typical session generally produces twice as many ideas as the more traditional method.

Mind Maps

Mind Maps let you see your entire knowledge of a subject laid out in front of you. This makes it easy to ensure you've covered the whole subject and not missed anything out, and you can see how all the different topics fit together. Mind Maps are also fantastic for generating ideas – you could easily come up with a hundred in a few minutes.

I produce my Mind Maps electronically these days, but let's start by doing things the old-fashioned way so you can see how they work.

You'll need a large sheet of plain white paper and some coloured pens or pencils. In the centre of the page, draw a small picture to represent your subject or idea. Use several colours, as this stimulates your brain to produce more ideas. Next, think about the main concepts that relate to your idea. These will be the main topics, chapters, key points or events in your book. Add each of these to the Mind Map as you think of them, forming a ring around the central picture. Draw a line from each item back to the central 'parent' picture to show where the idea came from. Some people like to draw a box around each item, but it isn't essential.

> Try using rolls of lining paper, found in the wallpaper section of your local DIY store.

Now consider each of these main concepts in turn and expand them outwards as far as you can. Add more ideas, related subjects, thoughts, concepts, properties, and so on, and draw lines to connect them. Use colours to show how different items relate to each other. Some branches will end up longer or shorter than others, but that's to be expected. If you run out of paper, tape another piece alongside.

Your brain prefers to work visually, so you might like to draw pictures or doodles of the objects or concepts as you add them. Spend time colouring them in and linking them to other objects, as this will help your brain to generate more ideas. As you start to see how things are connected and how the subject is organised, you'll gain a much better understanding of it, which will lead to yet more ideas. You'll probably find that when you start adding drawings and colours to your Mind Maps you'll need to use much larger pieces of paper – not because the pictures take up more space, but because you have so many more ideas.

When you've expanded all the main concepts as far as you can and added links between related items, your Mind Map is complete. You now have a summary of everything you know about that subject or story. Producing a complete Mind Map will take time, but look at how many ideas you produced. How long would it have taken you otherwise?

The modern way to create Mind Maps is to use computer software. This has several advantages. The page can be as big as you like, and you can expand branches as far as you like in any direction. You can collapse or expand branches to get a better view of what's going on. You can move branches around, or move items from one branch to another. As you add new branches, the existing ones move to create space, so your Mind Map always looks neat and organised. If you want to use pictures, you can choose from the hundreds supplied with the program rather than having to draw them yourself, or you can import your own. You can link items to other things, such as documents, text files, spreadsheets, charts, photos, or websites. And when your Mind Map is finished you can convert it into an outline and export it to your word processor.

> The software I use is MindJet MindManager 2002 – it came free with a computer magazine.

You can also use Mind Maps for learning, note taking and remembering. Find out more in *The Mind Map Book* by Tony & Barry Buzan.

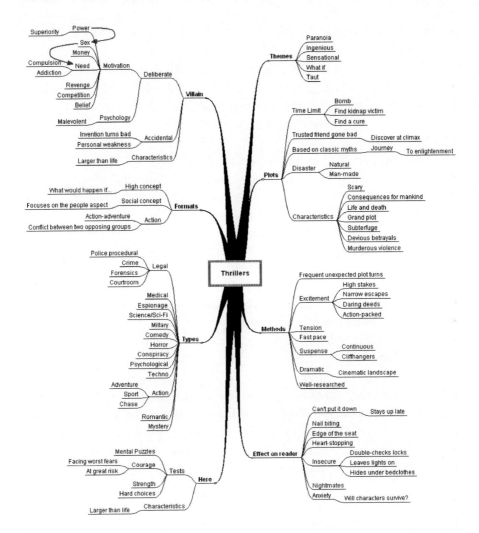

Figure 5.1: Mind Map

Clustering
Clustering is similar to Mind Mapping, but uses word-association techniques used by psychologists. He says "black", you say "white"; he says "wicked", you say "witch", and so on.

As you add each item, think about how it connects to the previous one and write the connecting factor on the line that joins them. If several items come to mind, add all of them. You can also link items to items in other branches, creating a web of links. Keep going for as long as you like. You're more likely to run out of time and paper than ideas.

The advantage of this method over Mind Maps is that ideas come faster and easier. The disadvantage is that the result is less organised and you'll have to reject more of the material at the critical review stage.

Key wording

Perhaps you aren't sure which word to put at the centre of your Mind Map. Maybe your word is so uninspiring that you can't get started. Here's how to get round the problem. Start by listing the key word(s) you need to find ideas about. Now look up each word in a thesaurus and write down all

> Microsoft Word has a built-in thesaurus. Press Shift + F7, or right-click on any word and choose Synonyms.

the relevant words that appeal to you. This will give you a more inspiring set of words to start from, and hopefully you'll find ideas popping into your head immediately.

Word webs

Word webs are similar to the Mind Mapping and clustering techniques above, but they're much better for generating story ideas.

Start by writing a single word in the centre of a large sheet of paper. You might like to choose a word that says something about you personally: creative, brain-dead, inspired, bored, busy, tired, happy, drunk. Draw six spokes radiating out from the central word to the edge of the page. Next – without thinking too hard – quickly come up with six more words you associate with that word. Put one on each spoke, about an inch from the centre. Now pick one of the spokes and follow it to the edge of the page, adding words that are associated with the previous one. If the central word was *conscientious* and the first word on that spoke was *careful*, you might end up with: safety, pin, needle, sewing, craftwork, hobby, amateur. Do the same for the other spokes. Now let your eyes wander over the page picking out words, or groups of words, or phrases, and see what happens. You'll find strange combinations that you'd never have come up with any other way.

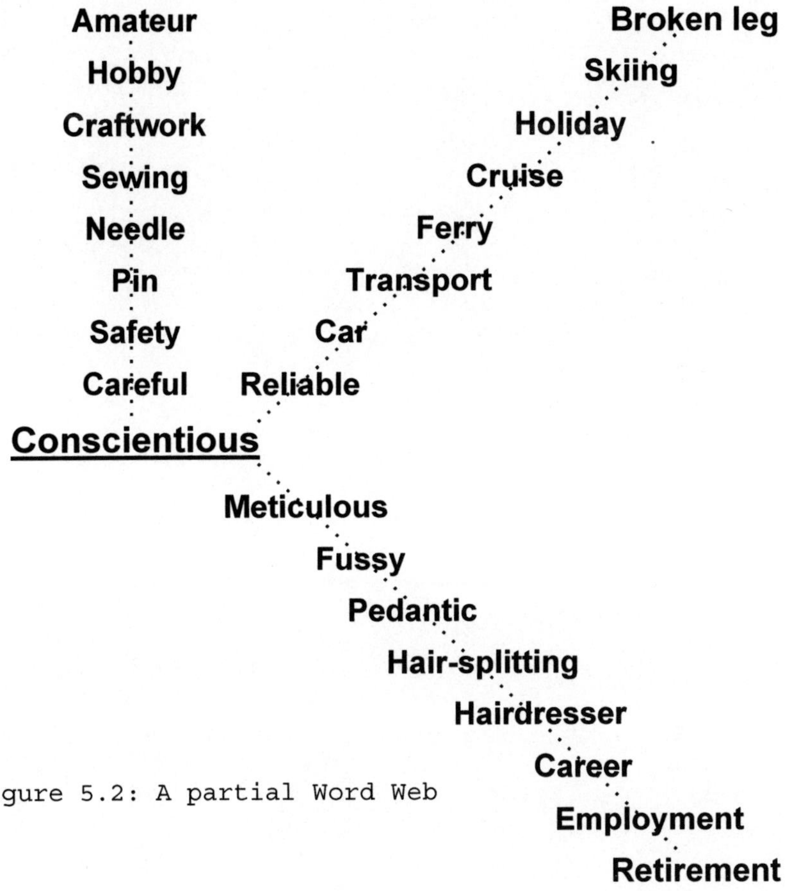

Amateur   **Broken leg**

Hobby   **Skiing**

Craftwork   **Holiday**

Sewing   **Cruise**

Needle   **Ferry**

Pin   **Transport**

Safety   **Car**

Careful   Reliable

Conscientious

Meticulous

Fussy

Pedantic

Hair-splitting

Hairdresser

Career

Figure 5.2: A partial Word Web

Employment

Retirement

What you don't know
The final step is to compile a list of all the things you need to research.

The next step
It's time to do some research.

6   Research

Traditionally, writers have been encouraged to gain as much knowledge as they possibly can about each subject they write about. The idea is that having an in-depth knowledge allows you to write with an air of 'authority'. You'll also collect more ideas while you research the subject, which can enhance the book, or lead the story in a new direction.

Unfortunately, much of what you learn won't end up in the finished book, so we're not going for the traditional approach; we don't have time. We won't be doing any more research than we need to. However, there are several techniques you can use to pick up information quickly and painlessly. This will give your writing more than enough authority to satisfy anyone that you're an expert in the subject.

In the previous chapter, you made a list of all the things you need to find out more about. So in this chapter you'll work through that list as quickly as possible. On the next few pages, you'll find research methods and information sources that should cover your every need.

Better note taking

Never skimp on your note taking by just jotting down a single word and hoping you'll remember what it means. You probably won't. Let's say you've just come across some old notes and found the word 'doors'. What was that about? It doesn't mean anything now. If you'd written 'door colours reflect your personality' or 'every closed door hides a mystery' then you'd know exactly what you meant.

Even though you're doing the research quickly, you should still cross-check every fact to ensure that everything you write is completely accurate. Don't guess, assume, make it up, or rely on a source you don't completely trust. It'll come back to haunt you later and you'll wish you'd done it properly.

Do the absolute minimum

Page after page of facts, descriptions and background information is boring, especially in fiction, and many readers will skip it. If you don't need it, don't bother writing it in the first place – and don't bother researching it either.

If you really must pack tons of information into your novel, weave it into the action and dialogue so your readers don't get bored and skip it.

For the fastest possible results, you should never over-research. Decide what information you need to tell the reader, how much you already know, then fill any gaps in your knowledge by reading, talking to friends, talking to experts, and the other techniques listed here. Then stop researching and get on with the writing.

All you're doing at this stage is filling in the gaps in your knowledge. If you come across anything completely new, save it for the next book. After all, if you're going to write a new book every couple of months, then you're going to need a heck of a lot of good material. If some of it's already maturing in your mind while you write the current book, then you'll have a head start when you're ready to write the next one.

Extra-value research

Why not research two or more books at once? Can you hold more than one book in your head at the same time? Of course you can. I've seen it written that you can't, and that you shouldn't do this. What rubbish! If you're properly organised and maintain separate sets of notes for each book, then it's very easy and saves a huge amount of time. And I'm certainly not going to turn away good ideas and research material just because it fits a project I've got planned for the future, rather than the current one.

Get involved with a website

A great way of finding out more about a particular subject is to set up a website on it. You'll soon get to know people's likes, dislikes and preferences, the questions that are most frequently asked, how much people already know, and so on. As your website becomes more widely known, people will come to you for information. They'll look upon you as an expert, send you press releases and new products to review, invite you to contribute to other publications, invite you to conferences and events, and much more. It's a fantastic way of immersing yourself in the subject.

You'll also find out who the experts are, build up a network of contacts, and discover the gaps in the market that you could fill. And your website is the ideal place to market your books when you've written them.

If you don't have the time, technical knowledge, or desire to set up a website, see if there's a good website that already covers the subject. Contact the owners to see if you could become involved as a volunteer. Many websites are understaffed and have a huge backlog of work and would appreciate the extra help. It's a great way of learning more about the subject in a very short space of time, and interacting with people who share your interest. You'll also enhance your reputation and build trust and expert status, which will be useful when you come to sell your book.

> Volunteers are *always* welcome at ideas4writers.co.uk!

Historical sources

Museums. Stately homes. Monuments. National Trust properties. Living museums and theme parks where people live, dress and work in period style. Historical societies will have historical records and picture archives, and many of them hold re-enactments in original costumes – great for photos. The Sealed Knot's website (www.sealedknot.org) will provide all the Civil War details you could wish for. They also hold battle re-enactments – another great photo opportunity. If you visit historic properties, don't forget to check the gift shop for useful mementos, guidebooks, postcards, and so on. These are especially valuable if photography is not permitted.

Also consider art galleries, art collections in books or on CD-ROM, biographies and autobiographies, and newspaper archives. Most town halls and local museums will have a collection of photographs showing scenes from the town's past, or they'll know someone who has such a collection.

The internet

The starting point of all internet research has to be the search engines, and by far the most popular at the time of writing is Google (www.google.co.uk). It's worth spending a few minutes reading Google's online help page and learning how to use the advanced search features. These will take you straight to the information you're looking for, rather than a huge list of websites that might possibly contain what you're looking for (but probably won't).

Other features of Google include the very useful *image search* and *groups search*. Image search is self-explanatory. Groups search means internet newsgroups, which are similar to the discussion forums found on many websites. There are thousands of newsgroups, covering every subject imaginable – and plenty more that aren't imaginable. Groups search lets you search these easily. and is well worth using if you don't find what you're looking for using the standard web search.

Other search engines include:

- AltaVista (www.altavista.co.uk)
- Ask Jeeves (www.ask.co.uk)
- DMOZ Open Directory Project (www.dmoz.org)
- WebCrawler (www.webcrawler.com)
- WebFetch (www.webfetch.com)
- Yahoo (www.yahoo.co.uk)

In fact, there are hundreds of different search engines, and as you become more proficient you'll discover which give the best results for the subjects you're interested in. Some Internet Service Providers, such as AOL and MSN, also have their own search engines. The Web-Crawler and WebFetch search engines are particularly interesting, because they send your query to several search engines at once and collate the responses for you.

Universities can be particularly useful as many of them maintain huge databases covering various subjects. As you carry out your research, you might be directed to a particular university database – and hopefully somebody will tell you who to contact to gain access to it.

Web logs or 'blogs' are a recent phenomenon. These are like personal online diaries where people write freely about their lives, interesting things they've come across, useful websites, trade secrets, conspiracy theories, rants and raves, inside news, and all sorts of things you'd never find anywhere else. Most of it is completely useless of course, but there's some good stuff out there if you're willing to dig. Blogs have come into their own during times of war and environmental disaster, allowing people in those areas to let the rest of the world know what's *really* happening. The Blogger website is a good starting point (www.blogger.com).

Internet Newsgroups and Discussion Forums

Newsgroups are one of the oldest parts of the internet, predating web pages. People with a common interest can post messages, see what others have posted, and post replies, building a conversation about the particular topic under discussion.

As I mentioned above, there are thousands of newsgroups covering just about every subject. Unfortunately, most of them are a complete waste of time. They're full of porn, spam, and people picking fights with each other, but very little actual information. There are a few good groups though, so it's always worth a quick look to see what's available for the subjects you're interested in. Most email programs, including Outlook Express, can be set up to access newsgroups. Your Internet Service Provider should provide instructions on their website telling you how to set this up. And, as mentioned above, you can also search newsgroups using Google's groups search facility.

The really good thing about newsgroups is that they aren't just passive information sources. Anyone can join in and post messages. If you've searched high and low and can't find the information you need, try posting a question on a relevant newsgroup. You'll usually get a same-day response – usually several responses all giving different answers.

One thing newsgroup users really hate is newcomers ('newbies') who keep asking the same questions. To combat this, most groups maintain a Frequently Asked Questions (FAQ) file. If you check through the messages in the newsgroup you should be able to find a copy of it. FAQs are particularly useful when you want to learn about a subject quickly. They contain all the information a newcomer to that subject needs, usually in a simple question and answer format.

If you don't find the information you're looking for in the FAQ, then you can assume it's safe to post a question without being yelled at. A good question to ask – if the answer isn't in the FAQ – is which are the best books and magazines on the subject.

The modern alternative to newsgroups are the discussion forums you find on many websites.

Interviewing

It's well worth learning how to interview effectively; you'll get better results faster. You need to know how to prepare for the interview, ask the right questions, steer the interview, make effective notes, deal with a difficult person, and – most importantly – why you're interviewing this person and exactly what you want to get out of it. There are many good books available, but you can't beat experience. Practise on your friends.

Libraries

Libraries contain two wonderful resources for writers: books and librarians. We've already discussed librarians in Chapter 4, so let's concentrate on books here.

See the sections on speed-reading and skimming, which will allow you to zip through a pile of books in no time.

When you're looking at books for research material, choose the ones with the best illustrations. Illustrations make research and writing so much easier; all you have to do is describe what you see. If you don't know what something is called, just describe it. If it's an item of clothing, the picture will show its colour, texture, how it's worn, and so on. If it's a tool, it might show how it's used, and the various parts might be labelled. A few good pictures might be all the research material you need to complete your book.

Whenever you use a book for research, make a note of the title, author, publisher, year of publication, and page number. This allows you to find the facts again easily, shows your publisher where you got the information from, and you can include the details in a bibliography section for readers who'd like to explore the subject further.

Also consider using children's books. These are great for a quick overview of a subject. And don't forget the British Library. See their website (www.bl.uk) for full details.

Local research

Whatever subject you're researching, you should be able to find someone not too far away who is an expert. It might be part of his job, in which case a browse through the *Yellow Pages* could prove fruitful. Ask friends, relatives, colleagues and teachers if they know of anyone who knows about the subject. You could also try the town hall, library, local studies centre, county records office, church records, and so on.

Often the best way to learn about a place is to ask the old folk who've spent their whole lives there. Pop into a traditional-looking pub and ask if there are any old regulars who come in each day. When you meet one, buy him a drink, explain what you want to know and why you want to know it, then sit back and listen. You might have to supply a few more drinks from time to time, but it's a small price to pay for the wealth of information he'll give you.

Most towns have local experts who know an enormous amount about the area and have access to all sorts of useful documents and archives. You can find these experts through your local Tourist Information Office, local studies centre, library, local college, or newspaper office.

Newspapers

Newspapers can serve many different purposes for writers – we've already considered them as a source of ideas. Let's say you're researching something and need information. Contact your local newspaper and tell them you're planning a book on whatever subject it is and you'd like them to print your request for information in case any of their readers can help. A week or two later you might well find yourself grinning cheesily from the pages of that very paper, next to an article about the book you're planning. With luck, you'll soon have more than enough information to complete the book.

If the information relates to another part of the country, contact the local paper for that region and ask them to print your request. They won't be quite so interested in you, so you probably won't get a photo, and the article might only be a couple of lines. But it's better than nothing.

Don't forget to let your local paper (and any others that printed your request) know when your book is published. You might well find yourself back in the paper and famous all over again. Make sure you tell them where their readers can buy your book from.

Other People

Other people can be so useful to you that this topic merits a whole chapter to itself. See Chapter 15.

Other People's Jobs

If you're writing about someone who does a particular job or follows a certain lifestyle, it's much easier and quicker to interview him at home or in his workplace than to spend ages making it all up from scratch and possibly getting it wrong. And it's much quicker than reading it all from books.

Make the most of your time with this person. Don't just ask questions. Look around and see what's going on. What sort of state is the place is in? Who else is there?

It's also interesting to try asking some controversial questions and see if he'll answer them. His refusal can be just as informative as a full answer. These sort of questions are best left until the end of the interview though, in case he decides to throw you out.

If you find someone who's very interesting and co-operative, see if you can arrange to spend a day shadowing him. See the section on job shadowing in Chapter 4.

Primary Research

This is where you become the source of the information rather than reading it somewhere else. Primary research can be expensive and time consuming, but sometimes it's the only way of getting the information you need. And at least you can be sure it's accurate.

Primary research includes conducting your own experiments, interviewing, market research, surveys and questionnaires.

Second-hand bookshops

Small independent bookshops and second-hand bookshops are well worth visiting. The people who run them usually know exactly what they have in stock, so ask them rather than searching yourself; they'll probably find what you need in a matter of seconds. Also try www.searchingforabook.com, which has an extensive list of second-hand books you can buy online.

Amazon (www.amazon.co.uk) now sells used books as well as new ones. This has expanded their range considerably and makes it much easier to get hold of out-of-print books. You'll also find a good selection of books on eBay (www.ebay.co.uk), the popular online auction site.

You can also use Amazon and eBay to sell your own books when you've finished with them. This is a great way of freeing up shelf space and recouping some of your research costs. Somebody might be desperately seeking a book that's gathering dust on your shelf, so do everyone a favour and put your unwanted books back into circulation.

> If you're interested in making some extra money, study the books that are sold on eBay and see how much demand there is for particular subjects or authors, and the sort of prices people are willing to pay. Scour jumble sales, charity shops, second-hand bookshops, house clearance sales, junk shops, car boot sales, and so on, looking for these titles, then sell them on eBay. There's a slight element of risk involved, which adds to the fun, but most books should fetch roughly the going rate.

Speed-reading

You can dramatically reduce the time it takes to carry out research by learning to speed-read. Speed-reading allows you to skip through mountains of books and research notes and locate the most useful material very quickly.

Speed-reading involves learning to see words as a group rather than as individual words. You go through the same process when learning to read – eventually you stop seeing words as individual letters and only see the words themselves. Speed-reading takes this to the next stage. It does take a lot of practice at first, but it soon becomes automatic, just like normal reading.

As an example, look at the individual letters that make up each word on this line. Now look at each word on the same line, seeing the whole words rather than the individual letters. Notice how much faster it is. Imagine if you could move up another level and see the same increase in speed. You can!

If you're interested in learning more about speed-reading, try *The Speed Reading Book* by Tony Buzan.

Skimming

If you can't speed-read, try skimming instead. Firstly, look at a book's table of contents. That immediately tells you which aspects of the subject this book covers, and you can jump straight to the topics you need to research. Read the entire table of contents, even if you're only interested in one or two topics, as this will give you a complete overview of this particular book's coverage of the subject in just a few seconds.

Next, flip through the book looking at section headings, sub-headings and chapter summaries. Again, I recommend skimming through the entire book, as the main points will stick in your mind. Glance through the index too if there is one.

The only parts of the book you should actually read properly are those that relate directly to the topics you're researching. However, you might well have picked up enough of the details already, just by reading the headings or chapter summaries.

You can easily get through a pile of books in minutes using this technique – up to thirty or forty books an hour with practice. Although if you pick the right books in the first place, then you won't need to read as many as that.

To help you choose the right books, go back to the list of words and topics you produced during the brainstorming and Mind Mapping sessions. Compare those words with the index of each book and see how many match. If there are several matches then that book is obviously worth studying further. If not, put it back on the shelf and try another.

Television

As well as the travel and documentary channels on satellite and cable TV, have a look at the Open University (OU) programmes that are shown late at night on BBC Two. These cover a diverse range of subjects, often presented by the OU's own lecturers – so you'll know exactly who to contact for more information. For programme schedules and other details, see the OU's website (www.open2.net).

The know-it-all friend

Everyone knows someone who's a bit of a know-it-all, with an opinion on everything. Ask him what he knows about the subject you're researching. If he doesn't know much about it, where would he start? What would he want to know? Where would he go to find out? Who would he ask? Does he know any experts in this subject? Or anyone who might have some experience in it? I'm sure your friend will be delighted to help. And it makes up for all those times when he drove you round the bend.

Travel

Friends who travel

Go through their holiday snaps, travel guides, souvenirs and so on. Ask them about their impressions of the places they've visited. If they're about to travel to somewhere you'd like to write about, ask them to take photos and bring back guidebooks and other useful souvenirs for you.

Language

Most readers will find it irritating if you fill your book with foreign words and phrases. If you're writing a non-fiction book and you use a foreign word, always explain what it means immediately. You only need a handful of foreign words to prove you know your stuff. In fiction, there's no need to have someone mangle English to indicate that it's not his first language. Simply avoid contractions such as *they're* or *aren't*, making his speech sound more formal, and slip in the odd foreign word or two where he doesn't know the English meaning. When you describe a foreign country in your novel, you only need to use three foreign words to prove you know what you're talking about. Obviously, you don't need to immerse yourself in the culture or learn the language if you only need three words; you can do it in a couple of minutes using a guidebook or phrase book. But you'd better make sure you *really* understand those three words.

Travel agents

The staff have probably been to many of the places you're interested in, so ask them questions. They'll also have a good selection of holiday brochures, travel guides, information for travellers to particular countries, and so on. It's worth checking their websites too.

Videos
Larger libraries usually stock a good selection of video documentaries and travelogues about foreign countries, cultures and people. Satellite and cable TV have several dedicated travel and documentary channels which also show these.

Visiting places
Going out and soaking up the atmosphere for yourself is one of the best and easiest ways of carrying out research. You can write far more convincingly about a place if you've actually been there.

Other sources of information
Tourist Information Offices, foreign embassies, British embassies in other countries, local and national newspapers and their websites.

Universities and colleges
Many universities cover specialist subjects or hold national archives on a particular subject. These are the places where experts in that subject are most likely to be found. Of course, you'll need to do a bit of research first to find out which universities specialise in which subjects, and to track down the names of the experts.

You could also try contacting your local college to see if any of the lecturers can point you in the right direction.

Universities and colleges have libraries, some of which are open to the public, although you might have to pay a fee if you're not a student. They usually have hundreds of specialist and technical books that you won't find in any public library, as well as research papers and other archives.

Your bookshelf
Every writer needs to keep a few books within easy reach. Start building up your collection now if you haven't already done so. At the very least, you'll need a good dictionary (not just a pocket one), a thesaurus, a style guide or a guide to English usage, and a quick guide to punctuation and grammar. An encyclopaedia is always useful too. I have the entire *Encyclopaedia Britannica* installed on my computer.

I also have a 'how things work' book, a 'how things are done' book, an encyclopaedia of science and technology, a book of quotations and a dictionary of popular phrases. You'll also want to add a few specialist books relating to your favourite subjects. In my case that's mostly writing, computing and technology, art, music, astronomy, and the paranormal.

Your job

It sometimes feels as if your job gets in the way of writing, but it doesn't have to be like that. We've already considered using your job as a source of ideas. And if you write about the people, places and situations you already know then you might not need to do any research at all.

Look at the people you work with and those who visit. Listen closely to the people who phone you. If you come across someone particularly interesting, change his name and there's a ready-made character. If your job involves travelling, look at the places you visit and the people you meet – all potential settings and characters for your book. You can do a surprising amount of research in company time, leaving your own time free for writing.

Other sources of information

There are thousands of other sources of information and it would be impossible to list them all. The information in this chapter should provide most writers with all the material they'll ever need. If you'd like to know more about researching, try Ann Hoffmann's book *Research for Writers*.

Use it while it's fresh

As with ideas, it's important to write everything down as soon as possible so you don't forget it. It's also a good idea to make a few additional notes about each item: who, where, and when – and how you might use it in your book.

The next step

You should now have all the information you need. In the next chapter we'll look at how to structure your book, organise it properly, and prepare a detailed outline to work from.

7 Planning and outlining

In this chapter, we'll refine your basic structure from Chapter 5 into a complete outline. You need it to be as complete as possible before moving on, because there won't be time to make any significant changes once the writing is underway. If you don't get the outline right now then you could end up having to cut some of your writing later. The time that went into producing that writing is then wasted.

You also need your outline to be as detailed as possible. Think of a TV programme or a movie where the camera cuts from one shot to another within the same scene. Ideally, you want each of those shots listed in your outline. You then know exactly where the story is going, you know it works, and you know it's complete. That makes it very easy and very quick to write. In the case of non-fiction, break things down in a similar way. You don't just want a list of chapters. You need a list of all the sub-headings and every item or topic that comes under them.

More detail now means easier writing later

If you lay out your book as a finely detailed outline before you start writing, you'll never have to wonder what you'll write next. You can't get stuck. You can't get writer's block. And if you get bored writing a particular scene or chapter, or find it too difficult, you can jump to another one instead. The beauty of a finely detailed plan is that you can skip about all over the place. Since you always know what you'll say in each section, all you have to do is write as fast as you can.

With a detailed outline of your entire book, your writing process goes something like this:

1. Read the outline and choose which section you want to work on next.

2. Spend five minutes thinking about exactly what you're going to write.

3. Write for between five and fifteen minutes and get that section finished.

You don't have to write or type – later in the book we'll look at several alternative methods.

You might write a single paragraph, or even a page or two, but it shouldn't be any more than that if you've broken your outline down into sufficient detail. When you've finished a section, go back to the outline and choose another one. Then repeat the process until the book is finished.

Introducing mini-sessions

By now, you might have spotted the big advantage of writing this way: no long writing sessions. All you need is five minutes to think about what you're going to write and a few more minutes to write it. You don't need to set aside several hours each day to write your book. A few minutes here and there will do the job nicely. You can fit in writing sessions whenever you have a few minutes to spare. For example, you might not have considered your lunch break long enough for a writing session. Using traditional writing methods, it probably isn't. Use mini-sessions though, and you could complete two or three pages during each lunch break. You could complete your entire book in three months writing only at lunchtimes. However, I suggest you spend an additional two hours writing each day and complete the book in a month.

As we've seen, these two additional hours don't have to be in a solid block. You could have a mini-session before you go to work. If you get a break at work, you could use that. If the rest of the family is watching TV and it's a programme you don't particularly want to see, slip away and do some more writing until the show is finished, then rejoin them. Have another mini-session before you go to bed. If you have to wait for someone and they're late, don't get annoyed or sit staring into space, use the time for another mini-session. Just make sure you have a copy of your outline and a notepad with you.

You can also think about your book while you're doing other things: walking the dog, putting up shelves, washing the car, and so on. All those things you usually associate with procrastinating suddenly become marvellous periods of thinking time. When you have everything straight in your head, write it down.

I'll discuss this in more detail later and suggest lots more pain free ways to fit mini writing sessions into your lifestyle.

The traditional way versus the modern way

Traditionally, an outline is a work in progress. It changes and evolves as you write the book. With our method though, there's only limited scope for such changes. The idea is that you work hard at making the outline as near perfect as possible in the first place and then stick to it rigidly. If you need to make changes, it's not too hard to move big chunks of text around in a word processor, especially if it's non-fiction. But making major changes partway through a novel is an altogether more serious business; you could spend days trying to reconnect all the joins seamlessly. Getting the outline right in the first place avoids this problem.

Some writers say write without an outline. Some don't even know what the ending will be. They just have a sort of idea of how to begin, and off they go. Perhaps something good will come out of it if they keep writing for a year or two – or perhaps not. That might suit some people, but it doesn't suit me. Nor does it suit the majority of professional writers; most bestsellers are planned in intricate detail.

Creating your outline

You'll need some software to create your outline. Many word processors have a built-in outline function. I'm going to concentrate on the one in Microsoft Word 2000. If you use a different program, you should find yours works in a similar way, although some of the commands may have different names or be in different places. If your word processor lacks this feature, there are several stand-alone outline programs available. At the end of the chapter we'll look at one called TreePad Lite, which is available for free.

Microsoft Word's built-in Outline function

Word treats the Outline function as another way of viewing a document. To access it, click on the View menu and choose Outline, or use the layout buttons at the bottom of the screen.

When you enter Outline View, a new toolbar appears.

Figure 7.1: Outline toolbar

The Outline function uses Word's styles to distinguish between the different heading and sub-heading levels. If you begin a new document and switch to Outline View, the style is set to *Heading 1*. You could now enter all the top-level headings (chapter names), pressing the Enter key after each one.

If you're not sure which button is which, hold your mouse pointer over each one for a couple of seconds and a label pops up to tell you.

If you want to insert a sub-heading, or turn a *Heading 1* (chapter title) into a *Heading 2* (sub-heading or topic heading), press the Tab key.

To turn a sub-heading back into a top-level heading, press Shift + Tab. You can have up to nine levels of heading, but most projects use just two or three. You could also use the backward and forward arrow buttons on the Outline toolbar instead of the Tab key.

The main text of your book will be 'body text', which uses Word's *normal* style. Since you're only preparing the outline at this stage, you don't need to add anything at this level yet. When you come to add the body text, you'll probably find it easier to come out of Outline View and use Normal View or Page Layout View instead. You can switch between the different views at any time.

If a heading has sub-headings or body text beneath it, a '+' symbol appears to its left. Double-click on this to show the lower levels. If something is hidden, a squiggly line indicates where it is.

You can reorganise the document very easily by selecting a heading and using the up or down arrows on the Outline toolbar to move it. If you've hidden everything except the top-level headings, then all the sub-headings and body text belonging to that heading move with it. If all the levels are on display, only the heading itself will move.

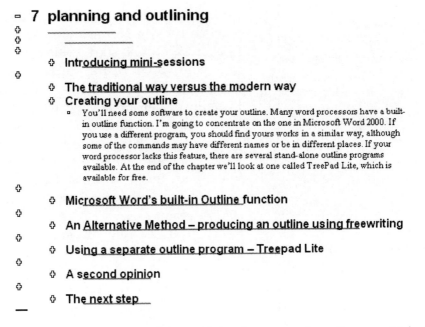

Figure 7.2: An example of an outline

You can easily control how many levels of heading are on display by using the number buttons on the Outline toolbar. For example, if you want to show headings 1, 2 and 3 and hide everything else, click the 3 button. To display everything, click the All button.

There's also a button to change a heading into body text. You can change it back into a heading again by using the backward and forward arrow buttons on the Outline toolbar.

When you print from Outline View, it will print whatever is actually on screen at that time. If some levels are hidden, they won't be printed. This makes it easy to print a summary of the entire document.

You should now create Heading 1 entries for each of the main branches on your Mind Map, or for each chapter in your book. Below each Heading 1, use the Tab key to insert any sub-headings for that chapter. Then add sub-sub-headings as required, or brief body text in the form of notes about the text you'll write later.

If you're exporting directly from a Mind Mapping program, then this stage has already been done for you. But you'll need to check the chapters are in the right order and rearrange them if necessary.

Here's a cheap way to get a full version of Microsoft Word if you don't already have it. Buy Microsoft Works Suite instead. Make sure you get the Suite version. This includes the full version of Word, plus several other home/office applications.

When you're happy with your outline, switch back to Normal View or Print Layout View and start writing the text of your book using mini writing sessions. All the headings and sub-headings will already be in place. If you want to alter the document's structure, go back into Outline View and change it. Make sure you set all your body text to *normal* style. This will ensure that you can switch between views seamlessly.

You can view any document in Outline View, but unless you've used styles to mark each level of heading and body text, it won't make much sense. Fix this by going back into Normal View and selecting a piece of text, then choose a style from the *styles* dropdown list on the Formatting toolbar.

The best way to learn how to use the Outline function is to play around with it. Create a test document that you can experiment with without worrying about causing any damage. Try switching between views to see how it looks, and practice creating headings, promoting and demoting them, turning them into body text, collapsing different levels, and moving things around.

Producing an outline using freewriting

In Chapter 5, we looked at using freewriting to create an overview of your book as if you were writing under exam conditions. You can use this as an alternative way of generating an outline.

Your overview should cover the entire book, complete with a proper beginning, middle and end. It should have a summary of all the topics to be covered, or details of the main storyline and sub-plots.

Break down your overview into a number of chapters. A good starting point is twenty to twenty-five chapters for fiction and ten chapters for non-fiction. Take your overview (or a copy of it) and draw lines across it to indicate where the chapter breaks occur. Then make a separate list of all the events or topics you'll cover in each chapter. Your overview might not be in the correct order at this stage. Some topics might appear under different headings, and some of the ideas from several different chapters might need pulling together under a single heading. Spend some time sorting this out. You might like to try a few alternative versions and show them to other people to see which they like best.

> How long should your outline be? That's entirely up to you. Mine are usually around one-tenth of the length of the finished book, so a 300-page novel will have a 30-page outline.

When you've finished, you'll have a set of chapters each containing a set of topics or scenes. Concentrate on a single topic or scene at a time and break it down into smaller and smaller chunks. Keep checking to make sure you've covered the subject completely and in as much detail as your readers expect. The more you can break the book down now, the easier it will be to write later. As we saw earlier, each item on your list represents a mini writing session that you should be able to complete with five minutes thinking time followed by no more than fifteen minutes of writing.

The better your outline is now, the easier and quicker the book will be to write later, so take as long as you need to get it right.

Using a separate outline program – Treepad Lite

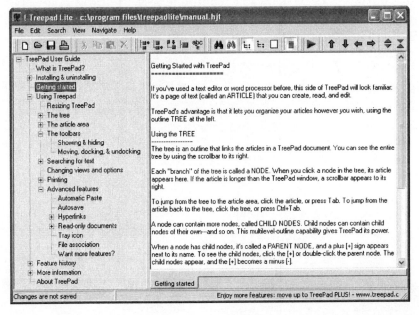

Figure 7.3: Treepad Lite

Treepad Lite works in a similar way to Word's outline function. Start by adding the main headings, add sub-headings below them, then add further detail below each of these. You're creating a tree structure, from which the program takes its name. In the screenshot, you can see the tree on the left. Each item on the tree has its own page – the large area on the right. Here you can add any notes you care to make about that item. You can put as much text here as you like, so you could write the entire text if you wanted to. (Most of us prefer to do this with a word processor though.)

When your outline is complete, you can export it as a text file, then open it up in your word processor to add the body text (if you haven't already done so).

Treepad Lite is free, but there are enhanced versions available for purchase, which include built-in word processing features, spell checking, the ability to insert graphics, and so on. For more details, or to download your free copy of Treepad Lite, see the Treepad website: www.treepad.com

A second opinion

Before you start writing your book, get someone else to read through your outline to check for completeness, glaring plot holes, improbabilities, and so on. Fixing the problems at this stage will be fairly easy. Trying to fix them when the book is finished will be a nightmare.

The next step

How on earth do you find enough time to write a book? We looked at one solution in this chapter – and there are lots more in the next one...

8   Finding time to write

Most of us already have hectic lives that are bursting at the seams. And now you want to write books as well? Let's make one thing clear: you never *find* time to write – you have to *make* time.

As we've already seen, that doesn't necessarily mean making dramatic changes to your life or giving up things you enjoy. By carefully budgeting your time, you can allocate it to things you have to do and those you enjoy doing and remove everything else from your schedule. Not only will you have more time for writing, but you'll be happier too.

For the time it takes to write your book, you must make writing your top priority. Everything else either supports your writing or gets in the way of it. Unfortunately, most of us can find lots of excuses not to write because we're too busy. So let's reverse that attitude: now you're too busy writing to do other things.

Budgeting your time

How do you spend your time at the moment? Keep a diary for a week, noting everything you do and how long you do it for: household chores, shopping, working, entertaining, watching TV, and so on. If you were watching TV, note the name of the programme too.

At the end of the week, add up all the time you spent on each activity. How much of the time were you being productive or enjoying yourself? How much of the time were you doing something out of habit rather than because you had to or because you enjoy it?

Now that you know how you spend your life, make a schedule showing all your busy times. Anything left over, even if it's only five minutes, can be allocated to writing.

Use a scoring system

As you look back through your diary, give each entry two scores:

- How essential was it?
- How much enjoyment did you get from it?

More time to write

Could you spend less time doing certain things and squeeze in a few mini writing sessions as well? Would you really miss something if you gave it up for just a few weeks to write your book?

End those lengthy phone calls

Do you spend hours on the phone? You must put your book first for a few weeks, so cut down on the phone calls or use email instead. Arrange to phone once a week to catch up with all the news, rather than every day. If you must call every day, try to keep it short; have a longer chat when you aren't writing. If you tell people you're writing a book and need time to do it, they'll understand. And it's only for a few weeks – unless you immediately write another book.

Speed-reading

We looked at speed-reading earlier. The ability to speed-read frees up vast amounts of time. It's particularly useful when researching, but you can also use it to read newspapers, reports, textbooks, minutes of meetings, research papers and anything else. If you speed-read at work, you'll have more time to do the work and you'll feel less stressed. That means you won't feel so tired when you get home.

Lots of little sessions add up

If you had fifteen minutes to spare, what would you do? Nothing very productive probably. Like most people, you probably think fifteen minutes isn't enough time to bother starting anything. It's not true.

One of the key points you should learn from this book is that it's more effective to spread your writing over several mini-sessions throughout the day than to have one long session. Finding the time for a long session can be difficult. But most people can find a spare fifteen or twenty minutes with little effort. And those mini-minutes sessions soon add up. You really can write your book without making any changes at all to your current lifestyle.

Use any spare time wisely by always carrying a notepad and pen, or a pocket computer. Always have a small section of your book in your mind that you can work on during idle moments.

Delegate

Do you have to do endless chores while everyone else slumps in front of the TV? That's not very fair, is it? It's time for a change.

The simple solution: get everyone else to do their share. Pay them or bribe them if necessary. Or go on strike until they start helping out. Tell them how much better things will be when your book is published. They could have a new house, a new car, a new TV, a new computer, a holiday in Florida... That should make them leap into action!

You don't have to delegate only your chores – they can help you with your book too. See Chapter 15 for details.

Before they have chance to lose their enthusiasm, draw up a rota and share out the jobs fairly between everyone. Then work out how much extra writing time you just gained.

Hired help

If you don't have anyone to help you with your chores, you could hire someone. Get a cleaner to come in twice a week, or a gardener once a fortnight. Use a laundry service. Most towns have someone who runs an ironing service. Have a look around and see what else is available. It's always best to get a personal recommendation from someone else who uses the service.

These services cost money, but they aren't terribly expensive when you consider the amount of extra writing time they give you. And you don't have to use them all the time. Just for the few weeks when you're writing.

Take time off

Is your day job getting in the way of writing? It shouldn't do if you stick to mini writing sessions. But if you need more writing time than your job allows, try taking a week or two off work.

Switch off the television sometimes

Try being more selective about what you watch on TV. How many programmes do you watch out of habit but no longer enjoy? Your writing should always come first. If something else is taking up valuable writing time then it has to justify it. A TV programme you watch out of habit and then moan about afterwards doesn't justify the time you spend watching it.

As I mentioned earlier, try keeping a TV diary for a week or two. Note every programme you watch and give it a rating, such as:

(a) Essential viewing.
(b) I could record it and watch it when the book's finished.
(c) Complete waste of time.

Ask the other members of your family which programmes you watch avidly and which ones you always moan about. If they're like most families, they'll know exactly what you watch and they'll have plenty to say about it.

Get out of your rut

Go back to your weekly schedule and have a look at the non-essential activities. You should already have considered dropping the ones you don't enjoy and cutting back for a few weeks on those you do. But what's left? Could it be done any faster if you did it differently? It's worth spending a few minutes thinking about alternative methods. You could also try talking it over with someone who isn't directly involved. They'll have a different perspective and might have some ideas that you wouldn't have thought of yourself.

Keep up with the news – faster

News reaches you in many different ways:

TV and radio programmes

You don't have to watch or listen to every news bulletin, and you don't have to choose the long news programmes – there are several five-minute summaries throughout the day. If there's a full-length news programme on, switch it off and come back for the summary at the end. If there's anyone else in the house, ask them to make a note of each news story and keep you informed.

Newspapers

Again, you probably read your daily paper more out of habit than anything else. If you want to know what's happening use Teletext, Ceefax, or the BBC news website: http://news.bbc.co.uk

Anything else – showbiz gossip, columns, articles and so on can wait until you have more time. Save your newspapers and go through them when your book is finished. That could be your reward.

You could also get friends and relatives to go through newspapers for you, clipping out anything particularly interesting or relevant. If they don't think it's relevant, you won't get to see it.

As you write your book, you'll probably start having ideas for the next one. Your helpers can go through the papers looking for material for you. You'll then have a nice pile of clippings waiting for you when you're ready to start it.

Magazines

You probably read these for entertainment, education or research. These things are not urgent. Let them pile up for a few weeks. Read them when you have time.

Email, ezines and newsletters

Email is easy to deal with: if you can't ignore it, delete it or file it away for later, then deal with it immediately. Most messages just need a very short response to say that you're engaged on a writing project and will reply more fully when it's completed. To save you writing this every time a new message comes in, keep a copy of it handy, then you can simply paste it in and hit the Send button. File these messages in a separate folder, then you'll know you need to send a longer reply later. In fact, it's a good idea to create several folders to hold the different sorts of message you receive. You can then keep your Inbox empty apart from the very latest messages.

> To create a new folder, right-click on your Inbox and choose New Folder. Give it a name and click OK. Now you can simply drag messages out of your Inbox and into your new folder.

Ezines (electronic magazines) and newsletters are easy to deal with: file them in their own folders until you have time to read them. If you receive any that you no longer read, unsubscribe from them.

Anything else

If you receive any other forms of news that I haven't mentioned here, you should be able to work out the best and quickest way of dealing with them. You might need to send a quick reply – have some already prepared. You might have to file it away for later – set up a simple filing system. You can probably throw away everything else.

Using your body clock

Work with your body's schedule rather than against it. When are you most awake, creative and alert? That's when you should be writing. Keep an hour-by-hour alertness diary for a week or two to find out when those times are. Set an alarm to go off every hour during the day, and make a note of how alert you feel at that time.

Can you adjust your daily schedule to take better advantage of your alert periods? That might mean getting to work earlier or later, taking lunch at a different time, or changing the family's meal times. You might need to get other people to agree to the change, but if you tell them why you're doing it and point out that it's just for a few weeks, that should persuade them.

You could also try writing when everyone else has gone to bed, or getting up an hour before everyone else. As we saw earlier, your morning sessions should be far more productive than late night sessions because you've just had a good night's rest. Even if you think you're a night person it's worth trying mornings for a week or two to see if you notice any improvement in your work rate.

How about those nights when you lie in bed and can't get to sleep? You may as well do some writing. You'll feel tired next day, but if you couldn't get to sleep then you'd have felt tired anyway. An hour of productive writing might be just the thing you need to help you sleep.

Do you have a lie-in at weekends? Could you skip it for a few weeks? That will give you several extra hours of writing time over the course of the month. If you write on a portable computer or use a pen and notepad, or if you dictate your book into a voice recorder, then you won't even have to get out of bed.

Work with other people's schedules

Study everyone else's routines and make a schedule showing when the best times for writing are. You might discover several writing opportunities you weren't aware of. They might only last for fifteen minutes or so, but, as we've already seen, that's all you need.

Make every minute count

Always go into a writing session knowing exactly what you're going to write. You'll already have the words in your head, so all you have to do is write them down. You don't waste any time getting warmed up, and you can't get writer's block.

Spring clean your life

If it only takes a month to write your book then there's no harm in postponing a few household chores. If you usually do something daily or every other day, perhaps you could just do it once or twice a week until the book is finished. If anyone notices the difference, ask them to do it for you while you get on with your book. How much extra writing time will that give you? How much sooner will you be able to finish your book? Every little helps.

Manage your time

If something will take a long time to do, it makes sense to leave it until you have plenty of time. When you have little time, do the shorter jobs.

If something urgent crops up, do it immediately. It gets it out of the way and it doesn't sit around cluttering up your thoughts. If it isn't urgent, postpone it until you've finished the current writing session or completed your book. Or delegate it to somebody else.

By reorganising your day, doing only what's absolutely necessary, and getting other people to help, you'll complete your work in double-quick time, leaving more time and energy for writing. When the book's finished, sort out the things you didn't do, and thank everyone who helped you.

Never a dull moment

One of the main problems with working on a long project such as a book is that your initial enthusiasm soon wears off. If your enthusiasm drifts a little, try working on several projects at once. If you use the methods in this book then this is perfectly possible because you'll have a great outline for each book. If you're fed up with writing and would rather spend the day editing, researching, or coming up with a plan for a fantastic new book you've just thought of, then do it. That way you'll never get bored and there will always be something interesting to do.

Save the planet – recycle

Let's say you're writing a novel. Most writers have a few unpublished stories tucked away, so how about reusing bits of them in your novel? If you already have a great set of characters, why waste time coming up with a new set? The same applies to the locations. You could even reuse bits of plot, or incorporate the original story into the novel as a sub-plot. If you write non-fiction, perhaps you have a few old magazine articles you could incorporate into the book.

You can even reuse your short stories and magazine articles if they've been published. Magazines generally only buy the right to use them once: First British Serial Rights (FBSR). Since you own the rights, you can reuse these pieces in your book without changing a single word.

Cross it off and start again

As soon as you complete a mini writing session, go to your outline, cross off the part you've just completed, and choose which section to work on next. Start thinking about that section immediately, even if you won't write it for a while.

Other ways of finding more time to write

When you aren't writing, you can still be thinking about writing: coming up with ideas, running sections of dialogue through your head, or thinking about the words and phrases you'll write in the next session. When you're watching TV or reading a newspaper you can look for ideas or do research at the same time.

You could also:

- Train yourself to write faster. See Chapter 13 for various ways of achieving this.

- Use technology and the techniques in this book to speed things up as much as possible.

- Don't use your writing time for anything except writing. Don't answer the door or the phone or your email.

- Get someone to take the children out for the day.

- Send the children off to stay with friends or relatives for the weekend.

- Turn down invitations to things you'd rather not go to anyway – your book is the perfect excuse!

The next step

It's nearly time to start writing your book. But how about doing a few warm-up exercises first? That's what we'll look at next.

9   Getting started

In this chapter, we'll look at some warm-up exercises you can do to ease yourself into a long writing session. If you've decided to take my advice and use mini writing sessions then you could skip this chapter. But it's only a short chapter, and I've thrown in a couple of extra tips along the way.

Editing comes later

Many writers begin a new writing session by re-reading the previous day's work and making corrections. That's a bad idea because it puts your brain into editing mode instead of writing mode. Editing is a completely separate process from writing and it uses a different part of the brain – logical rather than creative. When you eventually start writing, your brain will still be in editing mode and will be overly critical of what you write. You'll find yourself rewriting the same sentence over and over again and still not being happy with it. That's the sort of behaviour that leads to writer's block. You should forget all about editing, or making corrections of any sort, until the whole book is written. Then you can be as critical as you like. Chapter 18 is dedicated to the fastest ways of editing.

For now, avoid the temptation to re-read your work or make corrections and just carry on from where you left off in the previous session.

Perfection can wait

Many writers struggle to get past the first page because they know how important the first sentence needs to be. It's the most important sentence in the whole book. It has to hook the reader, the editor, the agent, and the publisher. So they spend days or weeks writing and rewriting that one sentence trying to make it perfect.

That's no way to work. Yes, the first sentence is the hardest to write, but you don't have to write it first. It's often better to leave it until the very end when you know exactly how the book turns out.

The first sentence should then be easy to write. In fact it'll probably be quite obvious what the first sentence should be. So for now, begin by writing: "This is a book about..." then come back and write the real opening sentence later.

Be excited

It's important to be excited about the subject or story you're writing about, as well as your book. If you can get to the point where you're completely absorbed in what you're doing, you'll find you have endless energy and enthusiasm for the work.

Be prepared

A great technique for clearing your thoughts and getting started is to concentrate on what you're going to write in the coming session, Make some rough notes or drawings or doodles. It's a useful way of generating ideas and organising your thoughts too.

Pick a word – any word

Pick a word from a book, newspaper, or magazine – it helps if it's a noun. Now write about that word for ten minutes without stopping. Describe its size, shape, colour, texture, smell, sound and taste. What does it remind you of? Who would use it? Let your mind wander, and write down whatever it comes up with.

Reverse psychology

Think about something you really *don't* want to write about. That immediately gives you a subject to write about. Start quickly, before your brain has time to object. Write whatever comes into your head, and keep going for several minutes.

Stop before the end

Some how-to books recommend stopping halfway through a sentence at the end of a writing session. You can then begin the next session by continuing the sentence, and you're immediately back into the swing of things.

This is very good advice, and it'll probably work for most people. But it doesn't work for me. If I didn't finish something, it would bother me so much that I'd have to go back and finish it. That would leave me with nothing to start on in the next session. So here's a variation that does work for me...

(Don't) stop before the end

At the end of each session, I finish everything that I meant to write, or I reach a convenient stopping point. If I'm writing fiction, I'll stop at the end of a scene. If I'm writing non-fiction, I'll stop at the end of a topic or sub-topic. I then write the first few words of the next session's work, followed by a few brief notes – just a line or so – to remind me what I'm about to say. In the next session, I pick up the thread of the work where I left it and carry on. Try this yourself if you find that stopping mid-sentence drives you nuts.

Having said that this technique works for me, that was before I discovered mini writing sessions of course.

The Ten-Minute Liar

Here's an interesting warm-up exercise. Spend ten minutes writing complete rubbish. Write anything that pops into your head: water is purple, wood conducts electricity, you can measure someone's intelligence by shining a torch up their nose, and so on.

You aren't trying to generate ideas, just getting your mind and typing fingers warmed up, but don't throw away what you write in these sessions. Maybe when you come to look at it again in a few months, you *will* see some great ideas there.

Vent your spleen

Sometimes you have so many other thoughts on your mind that you can't settle down and write. Perhaps someone cut you up on the motorway or upset you at work. You need to get these thoughts out of your system, so shut yourself away for five minutes or so with a notebook and really let rip. Write down all those things you didn't dare say at the time. Hurl insults at him, cast doubts about his parentage, accuse him of cheating on his driving test, and so on.

When you've calmed down, tear out the pages and put them aside to look at another day. You might find something useful that you can use in another piece of writing – especially if you need vicious insults!

The next step

Now that you're all warmed up and ready to go, it's time to knuckle down and get on with the writing.

10   Let's get writing

In this chapter, we'll look at the fastest ways to write the first draft of your book. There are several techniques here, and you certainly don't need to use all of them. Just pick the ones that appeal to you the most. If you try a technique and find it doesn't work for you, you'll find plenty more that will. And the one that didn't work for you will probably be the one that works best for somebody else. Let's get started...

Make a writing schedule

As we've already seen, you need to make time for your writing. A good starting point is to come up with a regular timetable for each week. Block out all the periods when your time is accounted for by essentials (and make sure they really are essential) and see what's left over. See Chapter 8 for more ideas about making time for your writing.

Write your book at lunchtime

This technique relies on you having a perfect outline, broken down into easily manageable chunks that each take no more than ten to fifteen minutes to write. How much you can write in that time depends on whether you write longhand or shorthand, your typing speed, and so on. We'll look at various ways of speeding these things up in later chapters.

Something to bear in mind if you're trying to write while you're at work: try to get away from your desk. You'll find it less disturbing and distracting if you take yourself off somewhere else. Try writing in a café, your car, the library, another part of the building, or go home if you live nearby.

Dictate it

Dictating your writing session into a digital voice recorder or personal tape recorder is a great alternative if you're in a situation where you can't write or type. It's a much faster way of getting the words down, so it's worth considering even if you are able to write or type. Recording your voice also means you don't have to be able to write in order to write a book. It doesn't matter if you're illiterate or dyslexic, so long as you can speak. Your words might need considerable revision and editing afterwards, but we'll address that later in the book.

The hardest part of the dictation technique is getting the words into written form afterwards. But you don't have to transcribe it yourself. See if you can persuade someone else to do it for you. This needn't cost you anything – you could arrange to walk their dog, mow their lawn, put up some shelves, or do their ironing in exchange. Think about how much time you'd save. Most people can speak 200 - 300 words a minute. I bet you can't type that fast!

If you can't find anyone to do the transcription for you and you don't have the time, inclination or ability to do it yourself, most towns have secretarial services where you can drop your tape in and have one of their staff transcribe it for you.

Another alternative, if you have a digital voice recorder, is to link it to your computer and play the recording into a dictation program that will transcribe it for you automatically. This can be a very cost-effective option – much cheaper than using a secretary. If you don't yet have a digital voice recorder, have a look at Dragon NaturallySpeaking 8 Mobile Edition. This popular dictation package includes a 'certified' digital voice recorder so you can be sure of getting good results. It can transcribe your work automatically with up to ninety-nine percent accuracy. It can also read your writing back to you, which is a great way of spotting mistakes when you're editing.

Just enough is good enough

There's no need to write everything out in full in the first draft. You can expand it all later and add any missing bits. There's no need to write in complete sentences. There's no need to complete words so long as it's obvious what you mean. Don't bother writing your characters' names out in full every time; just use their initials. Use as many abbreviations and shortcuts as you can. If you can't remember the exact word, leave a gap or put something roughly similar. You can look it up when you edit it.

No editing

Remember, this phase is all about writing. That means getting *roughly* the right words down in *roughly* the right order, with *roughly* the right spelling and *roughly* the right punctuation and grammar. You're not looking for perfection. Nobody else will ever see this version.

Don't bother to read what you've just written. If you can't help re-reading it and making corrections while you write, turn off your computer's screen.

You need to learn to ignore your internal critic who keeps telling you things such as: "you've used the wrong word", "your writing is no good", "your description doesn't make sense", and so on. There's a time and a place for editing, and this isn't it.

Beating negative thoughts

With our minds constantly flooded with thoughts about failure, you might feel tempted to give up whenever you get stuck. The best way to beat these thoughts is simply to carry on writing. One of the biggest secrets of getting published is PERSISTENCE.

It really doesn't matter if you think your writing is awful at this stage. It might well be awful, but it's only a first draft. It'll need a lot of polishing to turn it into something half decent. Getting a piece of writing finished is a triumph. And turning it into something great isn't particularly difficult – in fact, it can be a lot of fun. See Chapter 18 for full details.

Avoiding distractions

The last thing you want is to have your concentration broken by constant interruptions, so here are a few suggestions for avoiding them. If noise bothers you, you'll find some solutions for dealing with that issue in the next section.

(a) Wear a hat when you're busy. Make sure everyone knows that if you're wearing your hat then you're not to be disturbed.

(b) Stick a note on your front door asking people to go away or call back at a certain time. Hang 'Do Not Disturb' signs outside your writing room, and 'Quiet please, I'm writing' signs all over the house.

(c) Get someone else to look after the kids for an afternoon – you could look after theirs the following week.

(d) Turn on your telephone answering machine and leave a polite message saying that you're busy writing and you'll return calls later. Turn the phone's ringer off so you can't hear it.

(e) Prepare food in advance and put it in the fridge. Leave a note on the table telling everyone what it is, where it is, and to start without you if you're not there.

(f) Try going away for a few days on your own. Perhaps you could rent a holiday cottage out of season when it's cheap.

(g) House-sit for a friend or neighbour while they're away.

(h) Consider renting a small office or flat locally.

Noise avoidance strategies

Noise can be a real pain for writers. It can disturb your concentration to such an extent that getting any writing done at all becomes impossible. Here are a few solutions:

(a) Soundproof the walls of your writing room using special wall panels. Building and DIY suppliers sell these quite cheaply.

(b) Have double-glazing or secondary glazing installed if you don't already have it. If you can't afford to have the whole house done, just do your writing room.

(c) Try a pair of noise-cancelling headphones. These are readily available from hi-fi stores. Or you could use a pair of earplugs.

(d) Play tapes or CDs in the background to mask the noise. If music is too distracting, try natural sound recordings such as flowing streams, waves, birdsong, and so on.

(e) Try writing very early in the morning or very late at night when everyone's asleep.

(f) How about the ever-popular garden shed? If you want to work there during the winter, it's worth making sure it's weatherproof and well insulated. You might also want to consider installing electricity and heating.

(g) Have you considered a loft conversion? This will be expensive, but will add value to your house.

On the other hand, lack of noise can be a problem for some people. If you need to be able to hear something other than your own heartbeat and the whirr of the computer's fan, try playing tapes or CDs in the background.

Making non-writing time more productive

Use your non-writing time to think about what you're going to write next. Remember to concentrate on only one scene, section, sub-topic, or idea at a time. If you have any thoughts about things you've already written, make a note to change it in the second draft, but don't change it now. If you have ideas about sections you haven't written yet, attach them to the relevant part of your outline so you'll be able to find them easily when you get to that point.

Writing is a job

Try imagining that someone is paying you to write. He expects you to work at a certain rate, or at the very least to actually produce some writing. Otherwise you'll be sacked. Don't worry about the quality of the writing. Imagine that your boss employs an editor too. All you have to do is keep him supplied with rough text.

You could also try making your partner your 'boss'. He or she expects you to produce a certain amount of work in a given time – and you won't get your dinner until it's done.

Write every day

It's important to do some writing every day during this period, even if it's just one mini-session. If you miss a day, you'll feel guilty and you'll have to work even harder for the rest of the month to make up the time.

Turn off the spell checker and grammar checker

One of the major barriers to efficient writing is the spell checker that automatically underlines all your mistakes in red as you go. Your natural inclination is to stop and make the corrections there and then. If this is what you do, I recommend turning off the spell checker until you're ready to edit your work.

To turn off the spell checker in Microsoft Word: click on the Tools menu and choose Options, then go to the Spelling and Grammar page and remove the tick from the boxes labelled 'Check spelling as you type' and 'Check Grammar as you type'. Click OK to finish.

So many ways of saying the same thing

If you can think of several different ways of saying something, don't waste time trying to come up with the perfect sentence now. Just write down every version that comes to mind. By the time you come to edit that part, you'll have had time to reflect on it. The choice of words will seem much more straightforward.

Write a letter

If you're having problems, try writing a letter or email message to someone. Tell them about what you're writing – the story, the characters, the subject, or whatever it is. Most people find writing letters and emails much easier than *real* writing. And it's a great way of working out what the problem is and finding a solution. Of course, you don't actually have to send it.

Ditch the word processor

Here's another trick that will make writing seem easier. You're probably used to dashing off a quick email message to someone. If you're like me, these short notes sometimes turn into epic pieces of writing without you even being aware of it. What a great way to write!

Writing a message in Microsoft Outlook or Outlook Express is a lot less daunting than using a big scary word processor like Word. And there aren't any page breaks to worry you about how much or how little you've written.

If you have email at work, you could work on your book during breaks and quiet periods and send it to your home account. All those emails, together with the other bits and pieces of writing you do, will soon add up to a complete book.

Another approach

You could try writing your book in one-hour blocks. Set an alarm clock to go off in sixty minutes and stop when the time is up. If you're still in the mood to carry on, have a ten-minute break then start another sixty-minute session. Don't worry about how many words or pages you write in that time.

Remember those dreaded exams at school? You were probably able to fill page after page in just an hour or two. Perhaps you even ran out of paper and had to ask for more. So speed up your writing session by imagining yourself in an exam. Read the relevant part of your outline, spend a few minutes thinking about it and coming up with a plan, then dive in and let the words flow.

Goal!

You need something to aim for. A target. A milestone. A goal. Your ultimate goal is to finish the book of course, but that's too big and scary to start off with. Choose a smaller goal that you can complete in a single writing session, or in a day, or a week.

You need to make sure you've clearly defined and understood what your goal is. You'll also need to work out some sort of plan as to how you're going to achieve it.

A good goal should be positive – something you can look forward to achieving. It shouldn't be negative – something you *don't* want to happen.

Here are some examples of bad goals:

My goal is to write a book
Too big. You need to break it down into smaller goals that you can definitely accomplish. When is the deadline?

My goal is to write 50,000 words a day
That's a heck of a target and you stand very little chance of hitting it. Be a little more realistic.

I'll, um, you know, write some chapters and stuff, in a week or two
Too vague. How will you know when you've reached your goal?

My goal is to work harder
Another vague goal. What are you going to do specifically, and by when?

I will not write less than three pages per day
That's a realistic goal, but you're focusing on the negative aspects – 'not' and 'less'. Rewrite it to focus on the positive.

Here are some examples of good goals:

I will complete chapter three by Thursday lunchtime.

> Good goals are SMART: Specific, Measurable, Achievable, Realistic and Timed.

I will write at least three pages every day.

I will complete this topic by the end of the day.

All of these goals are achievable, they're specific, and they have a deadline. You'll know whether you've achieved them or not.

You might not achieve every goal, but that's OK. Goals should be challenging enough that you feel a sense of accomplishment when you achieve them. Most days you'll achieve your goal – and you'll feel great.

Charting your progress
A chart is a useful way of recording how well your book is progressing. It's really inspiring to see the lines on the chart building up towards your target.

You'll need to decide how you're going to measure your progress. Will it be the number of topics completed? Or the number of chapters? Or scenes? Or pages? Or words? Or will you use some other measurement? You'll also need to decide what your end target will be. How many topics are there? How many chapters? Or scenes? Or pages? Or words? And so on.

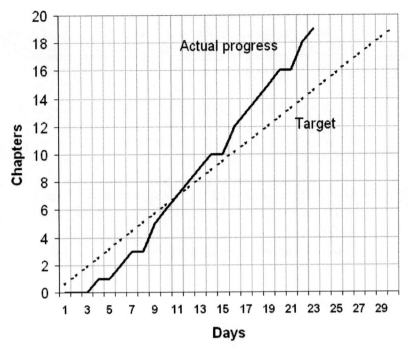

Figure 10.1 A completed progress chart

Ask for feedback

It's a good idea to get some feedback on how good your writing is. This terrifies most people, but if there's something wrong with your writing, it's far better to know about it now rather than later. That way you can correct your mistakes or study the aspects you're having trouble with, rather than writing an entire book that's completely unpublishable.

Here's how to get feedback:

(a) Let someone in your family read it, or give it to a friend. However, unless these people are writers themselves, they won't see the mistakes. They'll just tell you what a great writer you are and how much they loved reading it.

(b) Let another writer see it. There's probably a writer's circle near you that you could join. Most groups give you plenty of opportunities to have your work read and commented on by the other members.

(c) Try an online critique group, such as the one on ideas4writers.co.uk. You can post a short story or a few pages from your novel, and the other members will leave comments and advice.

(d) If you'd like a true expert's opinion, contact a professional editorial agency. They charge for their services, but you'll get detailed feedback and a fully corrected manuscript. Every writer should try this at least once. You'll find a list of recommended editorial agencies in Chapter 18.

A relaxing start

A good way to start a new writing day, or a long writing session, is to spend the first fifteen minutes relaxing, meditating, and concentrating only on your breathing. You should find that you can then recall that time of peace and silence at any time just by closing your eyes. But you need to have done the relaxation session earlier that day or it won't work so well.

The next step

In the next chapter we'll look at some techniques for writing fiction quickly. If you're more interested in non-fiction, you might want to jump ahead to Chapter 12.

11 Fast fiction

Tried and tested

Thousands of great stories have been written over the last few hundred years. The vast majority of them are long out of copyright and available for you to adapt in any way you wish. You can reuse the same characters, the same plots, the same events, the same locations – everything.

> 'Out of copyright' means that the author has been dead for at least seventy years.

Is there room for another retelling of *Romeo and Juliet*? Yes, of course. Give it a new twist. Make the characters executives in rival advertising agencies, for example. Give them modern names, a modern setting, modern language, modern problems, modern aspirations – the story practically writes itself.

Method acting

Get inside your main character's head (and body) and pretend to be him for a while. Walk around seeing the world as he sees it and feeling what he feels. Now, still in character, act out a scene from your story, pacing around the room and speaking the words. Have a tape recorder running to capture it all. You can then simply transcribe the recording. There should be very little need to edit these words; if you're properly in character, everything will be right first time.

Try stepping into the villain's body too. The world should seem very different now. The more characters you can step into, the faster and easier your story will be to write.

If you'd like to learn more about method acting, try taking an acting class, or reading Konstantin Stanislavsky's book, *Building a Character*.

If you're having trouble making your characters different from each other, make a list of five good points and five bad points about each of them. Make sure that at least three items on each list are unique to that character. It's also a good idea if one item is the same as another character's so they have something in common. If the hero has something in common with the villain, for example, that could make for a very interesting story.

Another point to remember is that no one is wholly good or wholly bad – except in fairy tales and pantomimes.

Knowing your genre

If you're writing a genre book – romance, fantasy, horror, science fiction and so on – it's important that you know that genre inside out. There are plenty of guidebooks available, but you should also read stories by as many different writers in that genre as possible. You need to be fully familiar with all the tricks, conventions and stereotypes the reader will expect to see.

You could also find some websites dedicated to your chosen genre and see if they give an overview of what it's all about. The more you know about your genre, the faster and more accurately you'll be able to write it.

Write about what you know

As far as this book is concerned, 'write about what you know' simply means: if you know about something then you can write about it quickly and authoritatively without having to do any research.

Write about your own life, things you've seen, things that have happened, people you've met, the place where you live, other places you've visited, and so on. Remember how you felt at the time and try to recall the atmosphere and mood. Use the knowledge you've gained from your job and your hobbies. Use what you read in books, magazines and newspapers. If you can still remember something you read about several months ago, then it must be interesting enough to write about.

Let it grow

It's a good idea to let a new story grow for a while, preferably for several months. Make a note of any relevant news items or websites you come across during this period. You might have been writing other books during this period, so by the time you start writing this new one it might have been developing in your head for a good three months. Start doing the brainstorming, Mind Mapping, outlining and research. It'll all come together remarkably quickly.

Let the characters take over

Sometimes, when you have exactly the right characters and exactly the right situation, something miraculous happens and the fictional characters come to life. They take over. You can hear them and see them. All you have to do is let them get on with the story and follow along, writing down everything they do, say, and feel.

The secret of success here is to have a rigid outline and insist that the characters stick to it. They still have a free rein to say what they like in their own words. If any of them objects then he's either the wrong character for that story or you're forcing him to do something out of character. You'll need to make some rapid changes to fix the problem: set the story somewhere else, modify the character's personality or background, change the way he responds to the problem, pass the problem onto a different character, or replace him with someone else. However, if you've let the story and characters grow for a decent period before starting to write it then you shouldn't ever have this problem

Match your mood

Try to synchronise your writing with your mood. Write sad bits on sad days and happy bits on happy days. Novels generally include a wide range of emotions. For maximum impact, you should feel those same emotions at the same time as you write them. It's very difficult to write a sad scene when you're in a jolly mood. You'll have to work so much harder to recreate feelings that come naturally if you wait until your mood changes.

Life is a buzz

Writing can be a lonely business. If you're the sort of writer who shuts himself away for hours on end then you'll have to get used to this. But if you use the mini-sessions technique, you can still join in with everything that's going on. As a result, your writing should be much livelier, especially the dialogue.

Earlier, we talked about spending the first week gathering ideas, planning, researching and outlining your novel. It's a great idea to spend as much of that week as possible immersed in the buzz of life. Go to parties, read books, newspapers and magazines, watch lots of TV, listen to the radio, go to the movies, catch up on your 'social' emails and join in the conversations at work. It'll be a hectic week, but you can have a nice rest when you start the writing.

Picture this

You can describe things more easily if you can see them right in front of you, rather than having to remember or imagine them. Surround yourself with as many relevant objects, photos, drawings, maps, doodles, sketches and so on as you can lay your hands on.

Search for pictures of your characters in magazines and mail order catalogues. Now, whenever you need to describe them, you don't have to look through pages of notes; they're right in front of you. If you can't find any pictures, try drawing them. Nobody else needs to see your drawings, so they don't have to be accurate. They don't even have to look real: if someone has a square face, simply draw a square; if it's heart-shaped then draw a heart. So long as you understand what each part represents, that's good enough. If you think your drawings look 'stupid', ask a friend who's good at art to draw them for you.

Similarly, look for photos of the locations where your story is set – or locations that *look similar*. Even if it's a faraway place, you should be able to find photos in books or magazines or on the internet.

You might also like to consider making a storyboard of your novel. That means sketching a representation of each major point in the story on separate pieces of paper. It's useful to have a large wall to stick all these pieces of paper to. You can then reorganise them easily as you try to make the story flow. Again, it doesn't matter if you can't draw, because nobody else needs to see them. You could also use a computer graphics program and clipart. If you don't have the right clipart image, use Google's image search facility to find something suitable, then copy and paste it into your picture – if no one else will ever see your storyboard then you don't need to worry about copyright.

Cull the dull

If any of your characters seem too dull, you could simply drop them from the story and find some more interesting ones to replace them. That takes time though, so how about keeping your current set of characters but digging up a few dark secrets from their backgrounds to add a little spice and intrigue? Or you could replace the weakest character with one you used in another story. Another alternative, if you don't mind drifting away from your pre-planned outline, is to kill him off. And show his death in the story – that'll make a lively scene.

A sense of purpose

Every story needs a purpose. It might be to entertain, to move, to educate and inform, and so on. It's a good idea to write down exactly what your story's purpose is before you start writing it. Whenever you find yourself getting stuck, not knowing where to go next, a quick glance at your statement of purpose will remind you of what you're trying to achieve.

This is your life

Use as much of your own life story as you feel comfortable with. Your own experiences will come across on the page as being very real without you having to do too much work. If you need your character to experience pain, for example, recall a time when you were in severe pain and describe how you felt. Perhaps your main character shares some of your own personal history – it's much quicker than inventing it. What memories do you have of the events that shaped your life? What were the key turning points and little details that made you into the person you are today? Give your character a few of those same memories, or spread your experiences among several characters. Use events from your dreams and nightmares too, or let your characters have the same dreams and nightmares as you do.

It's worth bearing in mind that nothing should appear in your story unless there's a reason for it – and that applies to dreams too.

Creating a character from your own memories

- Who or what did you want to be when you were growing up?

- What were you most scared of as a child?

- What are you most scared of now?

- What do you wish for?

- What are the biggest mistakes you've made?

- Think about the times when you failed. Did everyone else know, or did you manage to get away with it?

- What lies do you remember telling?

- What have you done that you now regret?

- What did you not do and now wish you had?

- What makes you cringe with embarrassment?

- What was the bravest thing you ever did?

- Who have you loved, and who have you hated? Why? Did love ever turn to hate? Did hate ever turn to love?

Speeding things up

If you're writing an action-packed scene, you need the story and dialogue to speed up. Here are a few tips on how to do that:

(a) Focus on the current action and forget about other details for now. If armed baddies are chasing your hero, his only concern is getting away. He won't be wondering whether his brother's house sale went through on time.

(b) Imagine you're filming the action with a video camera. Show the fine details in close-up – the sweat on the hero's forehead, anxious glances in the rear-view mirror (or what's left of it), frantic pounding on the horn, the low fuel light flashing, and so on. Everything else is just a blur – and if he doesn't notice it then you shouldn't mention it.

(c) Keep your sentences short and stick to just verbs and nouns. Make those verbs and nouns as specific and vivid as possible.

(d) To speed up dialogue, don't mention what the characters are doing as they speak.

(e) Stick to the point. The characters need to get the facts across to each other quickly and start forming a plan. They don't have time to reminisce about a similar case they were involved in years ago.

(f) Start in the middle of the conversation and get straight to the point. Leave out the beginning where everyone introduces themselves. End the scene as quickly as possible. That might mean cutting off the end of the dialogue. Maybe the hero suddenly dashes from the room shouting his thanks and heads off to continue his adventure.

(g) When someone is talking fast, thinking about other things, and only half listening to what the other person is saying, things can get a little confused. People talk at cross-purposes. Words come out wrong. Only later, when things have gone badly wrong, will our hero run the conversation through his head again and realise what the other person *really* meant.

Slowing things down

(a) To slow down the action, take time to describe the surroundings. As before, imagine you're filming the scene, but taking panoramic and group shots rather than extreme close-ups.

(b) Use longer sentences, and drop in a few descriptive adverbs and adjectives where necessary.

(c) Let the characters catch up on things that have been happening elsewhere. They have time to analyse where they went wrong and make new plans.

(d) Include a love scene.

(e) To slow down dialogue, show the entire conversation: beginning, middle and end.

(f) Let the characters talk around the point and discuss other issues, reminisce about previous adventures, tell jokes, and so on. But remember, these seemingly pointless conversations must be there for a purpose. Use them to:

- Convey extra information.
- Hide clues and red herrings.
- Reveal something new about a character.
- Emphasise certain aspects of a character's personality.

Common sense(s)

As you write your novel, keep in mind the five senses: sight, sound, touch, taste and smell. They add so much to the realism of a scene. Many writers concentrate on sights and sounds and forget all about the other three. The *best* writers use *all* of them.

Essential writing skills

To write quickly, you need to be confident in your writing ability, and that means acquiring the essential skills:

- Characterisation
- Plotting
- Dialogue
- Description
- Viewpoint

You'll also find it useful to study:

- Pacing
- Conflict
- Action and suspense
- Theme
- Structure

These are all learnable skills and it doesn't take long to learn the basics. A decent creative writing course should cover them all and give you plenty of opportunities to practise them and get feedback and advice.

You'll also find plenty of books that cover these topics in detail. I can particularly recommend *The Creative Writing Coursebook* edited by Julia Bell and Paul Magrs.

Stay with the action

If your main character is lying in a hospital bed, he can't really be involved in the action for a while. So this is a good time to switch to another character's point of view. This adds variety and makes the story more interesting to read – and more interesting to write. And that means you'll write faster.

Heroic myths

Here's a fantastic shortcut for creating a great structure for your novel. Get yourself a copy of Joseph Campbell's book *Hero with a Thousand Faces*. This looks at the mythological hero and his adventures, and relates them to modern stories, which, surprisingly enough, often follow *exactly* the same structure.

A typical myth concerns the hero who's summoned to go on an adventure but is reluctant to do so. He's urged on by a mother or father figure and eventually agrees and is given aid. Along the way he encounters many setbacks and his skills are well tested. He might become despondent, but eventually overcomes the problem with a combination of ingenuity, bravery, trickery and quick thinking. He often has a female to help him. He achieves his aim and gets his reward. His achievement helps the world and enhances his own reputation.

Did that also sound like a modern story structure to you? It should do. Think of any of the James Bond movies, Lord of the Rings, Star Wars, Indiana Jones, and hundreds more. Let's use that outline for a typical James Bond adventure. The hero (James Bond) is summoned (from a luxurious holiday) to go on an adventure (to recover a stolen computer chip) but is reluctant. He's urged on by a mother or father figure (Moneypenny and M) and given aid (gadgets).

The story has hardly started, but it's already clear that it fits the structure of a myth perfectly. Why not save yourself time and effort and use heroic myths as the basis of your novel? I urge you to read

Joseph Campbell's book and apply what you learn to your own writing. After all, this structure has stood the test of time for thousands of years – you're *guaranteed* a great story. And with no need to work out a structure for your novel, you've just saved yourself a lot more time.

Magic formulas

The heroic myth is an example of a formula. Some writers despise formulas, but I love them; they're fantastic tools for creating great stories quickly.

Using a formula certainly does not mean that every story you write will be identical. A good formula is tried and tested and very flexible. You can reuse it time after time, simply slotting in new characters, locations and situations. And, as we saw with heroic myths above, if you stick to the formula then you're guaranteed a great story every time.

You'll find an excellent formula for writing novels in Evan Marshall's book *Novel Writing - 16 steps to success*. In fact the whole book is one big step-by-step formula. Each step is carefully explained so you always know what you're doing, why you're doing it, and what effect it will have on the story.

I was delighted to note that my latest novel adheres to the Marshall formula pretty well – and that was before I even read the book. Having studied the formula, I realised that I needed to introduce an extra character and make a few other changes. But it's undoubtedly made it a better story and opened up new possibilities I hadn't considered before. I'll be using it for all my novels from now on.

Make it real

By far the quickest way of writing a novel is to use characters, locations, situations and dialogue that are real. That means using people and places you know, events you've personally been involved in, and dialogue you've overheard. Let's look at each of these in more detail.

People

Using real people can be dangerous, especially if you place them in disparaging situations and they recognise themselves. They could sue you for libel. You obviously don't ever use their real names unless they've given their permission. You can construct characters using elements from several different people: your manager's temper, your cousin's cowardice, your neighbour's fondness for guns, and so on. Include something of yourself too, so you have some sort of empathy with each character. What do they look like? Again, take bits and pieces from different people you know, or base them on someone you saw in the street or a photo in a magazine.

> Some people would love to be in your books and would be happy for their character to be involved in anything – the more scandalous the better!

Places

Use your own town, city or neighbourhood. You probably know the place inside out, so writing about it will be easy and you won't need to do any research. Don't worry that it'll seem too 'ordinary'. It'll still sound interesting (or even exotic) to everyone else. And the people who live there will all want to read your story to see if they recognise anyone.

If the place really is deadly dull, make that a feature of the story, or gloss over the setting and concentrate on the characters and the action. If you need to include somewhere exotic, use somewhere that you've been on holiday.

Events

Here are a few to get you thinking:

- Holidays – especially holiday disasters.

- Romantic dates that went wrong.

- School days.

- Childhood adventures.

- Jobs you've had, and the strange things that happened there.

- Work colleagues who did strange things.

- Accidents you've had or seen.

- The times when you've been drunk.

- Times when you've been happy, angry, sad, jealous, and so on.

- Births, marriages and deaths.

- Successes and failures.

- Arguments.

- Christmases you'd rather forget.

Dialogue

Always make a note of any great lines you hear. Edit out the pauses, repetitions, "ums" and "ers", and so on. If it's a joke or one-liner, find a way of working it into the plot. If someone has a strong accent or dialect, don't waste time trying to imitate it. It takes too long and readers hate it. Just say that he spoke with a strong Scottish accent. You can add a foreign word or two for colour, but don't use any more than that. Sometimes changing the order of the words can be very effective too. But if you aren't sure, just write it in plain English.

Listen to other people's conversations whenever you can – but pretend to be engrossed in something else. Listen to conversations at work, especially if one of your colleagues takes a phone call from someone with a complaint, or if he gets told off by the boss. Try to get involved in all the gossip.

If people know you're a writer, they're likely to clam up when you're around. The simple solution: don't tell them you're a writer, or write under a different name.

Don't spoil the broth

Use the minimum number of characters you can get away with. You don't want to waste time coming up with new characters and preparing background histories, motivations, goals, and so on. If one character can have several different functions, do it that way rather than having lots of minor roles. Think of a bodyguard who also works as a doorman at night, coaches the school football team, gives the church service on Sundays, and cuts hair for a hobby. You could have given those roles to five separate characters. Instead, you now have one *very* interesting character who can play a much bigger part in your story.

Naming your character

By far the easiest way of coming up with a name for your character is to use the ideas4writers.co.uk Name Engine.

Other methods include picking them at random from telephone directories, books of baby names, gravestones, credits from movies (especially useful for foreign names), and so on. A good way of finding surnames is to use street names from the *London A-Z*.

Give your characters any old names to get the story started. Their real names will come to you later when you know them better. You could even call them by their role rather than by name – Hero, Lover, Best Friend, Villain, Boss, and so on. Or use descriptions: Lonely Co-worker, Hunky Friend. Or think about the movie version of your novel and use the names of the actors you'd choose to play them.

No need to rush

If you think writing an entire novel this quickly is challenging, spare a thought for the 300 or so brave/foolhardy souls who enter the International Three-Day Novel Contest each year.

But wait! Those three-day writers routinely use a few cheats. Firstly, they're allowed to prepare an outline in advance. Secondly, they don't have to produce a polished piece of writing, only a rough first draft. And thirdly, they're allowed to work in pairs or groups.

But there's nothing to stop you from using all those three-day writing cheats too – and many more. In fact cheating is positively encouraged – so much so that I've dedicated Chapters 14 and 15 to this very topic.

The next stage

In the next chapter we'll look the fastest ways to write non-fiction books. Feel free to skip to Chapter 13 if that doesn't interest you.

12 Fast non-fiction

In a non-fiction book, it's the quality of the information that counts. It helps if it's well written and fun to read of course, but your amusing anecdotes and jokes are worthless without complete accuracy, meticulous research, and at least some information that can't be found in any competing title.

Sell it first

Unless you're planning to self-publish your book, it's a complete waste of time to begin writing it until you have a contract. Instead, concentrate on coming up with great ideas, researching the market, preparing outlines and synopses, and submitting query letters and proposals to publishers. Some people recommend writing one or two complete chapters to give an idea of what the finished book might look like, but I wouldn't even do that unless a publisher saw potential in my idea and asked me to provide them.

Depending on your experience, qualifications, market research, and the quality of your ideas and proposals, you might have to submit twenty or more proposals before you get one accepted. If you'd written those twenty books and then found that no publisher would take them, you'd have wasted years.

Are you an expert?

My definition of an expert is someone who knows enough about a subject to be able to teach it as an evening class. If you feel that you could do this then you're enough of an expert to write a book on it. If not, then you still have some learning to do. There's nothing wrong with learning more about your subject. It increases your expertise and your marketability as a writer, and provides valuable material for your book. If you're particularly interested in the subject, you'll be keen to learn more anyway.

But what if you spot a gap in the market for a book on a subject you don't know well? You'd love to write the book, but it would take far too long to build up the required level of knowledge. In this case, the sensible option is to find somebody else who is an expert and persuade him to work with you.

See if you can find someone who currently teaches the subject. Check the evening class schedules at your local college or ask the teachers at your local school. They might not be interested themselves, but they might know someone who is. Also try the lecturers at your nearest university, or look for someone who works in that field. Ask your friends, family and work colleagues to help you in your search.

Use the internet too. Whatever your subject, there are probably several websites dedicated to it, and you should be able to contact experts and enthusiasts through these, or at least find out who those experts are.

You could go to a gathering of experts – a seminar, exhibition, or conference, for example. One trip should provide all the information you need for your book, and hopefully you'll come away with a few useful contacts too. A day well spent.

Once you've found your expert and persuaded him to work with you, there are a few more issues to deal with. You'll need to discuss who does what, whose name will be on the cover, how disputes will be settled, how royalties will be split, and so on. Get this in writing as soon as possible as it will save a lot of argument and frustration if anything goes wrong.

Broad or narrow?

Some subjects are too big to cover in a single volume unless you're writing a simple overview for beginners.

If you're planning to write about a large subject, you could split it into small topics and find separate experts for each of them. You could even make each topic into a separate book and create a series that covers the subject in depth. It all depends on how big the subject is, how many experts you can find, and what readers are prepared to buy.

Let's take the subject of gardening as an example. You could start by writing a beginner's guide aimed at new gardeners. That would fill one book very nicely. But then you might decide to write a more detailed version for more experienced gardeners. That's a nice idea, but you soon realise you'd need thousands of pages. Fortunately, gardening is easy to divide into separate topics and you can write a book about each of them:

- Garden tools and their use, maintenance and repair.

- Trees and hedges.

- Shrubs and borders.

- Fences, gates and other woodwork.

- Patios, paving, walls, barbecues and other stonework.

- Lawns.

- Flowers.

- Vegetables.

- Ponds and water features.

- Pests and diseases.

- and many more

Your extensive knowledge of gardening now fills an entire shelf.

How big is your specialist subject? How many different topics are there? Could you come up with enough information on each topic to fill an entire book? Could you combine several smaller topics into a single book?

Find out what books are already available. Are some topics well covered? Are any not covered? Could you write a better book, or approach the topic from a different angle, or aim it at a different audience?

Adding value to your book

Ask experts what they've learnt about the subject that the guidebooks never mention. You'll hear plenty of lively anecdotes and collect some great material for your book that isn't available anywhere else. If you're going to write a book, make it the best.

Consider adding a resources section at the back of your book. They're quick and easy to produce, and for many readers they're the most useful part of the book. They really do add significant value to your book. Adding value is a good thing because it makes your book easier to sell when potential buyers realise how much more they're getting for their money.

What should go in your resources section? Start with a bibliography – books and magazines you referred to when writing the book. Add a further list of recommended books, magazines, websites and newsgroups for those who want to take the subject further. Give details of organisations readers can contact or join. If you mentioned any products, list these along with details of the suppliers or manufacturers. If you've mentioned things such as free software utilities, list these too, including details of where readers can download them from.

Give them what they want

When people buy a non-fiction book, they usually want to know how to achieve their goals with little or no effort on their part. Someone with poor drawing skills, for example, hopes to turn into a great artist just by reading your book. So it's a good idea to include as many shortcuts, handy hints, instant skill ideas, inside knowledge, tips of the trade, and zero-maintenance solutions as you can come up with

Whatever subject you're planning to write about, there's probably a magazine that covers it – and probably several. Most magazines have a section where they answer readers' questions. This is valuable information because it tells you what people want to know. You should be covering these very same things in your book.

Cheat number one – rewriting other people's work

Collect as many of these questions and answers as possible from a variety of magazines so you get different levels of expertise and different angles. Ideally, your collection of questions and answers should span at least a couple of years worth of magazines, so it's worth tracking down as many back issues as you can find.

Once you have plenty of questions, sort them into topics and link them together to form an orderly structure. You'll probably need to write a few more questions and answers of your own to fill the gaps.

Putting a book together this way should be a very quick exercise. Of course, you won't ever use the actual questions and answers you clipped from the magazines – you'll have to write your own versions to avoid infringing their copyright.

Another method is to collect just the questions. This forces you to research and write your own answers and is a great way of testing your knowledge. However, as a time saver I'd collect the answers too and rewrite them in my own words. I recommend double-checking the answers though, as magazines sometimes make mistakes. Their answer might not be the only one, nor might it be the best. Check the readers' letters pages in later issues to see if anyone sends in a better solution.

Can I ask you a question?

Another way of finding out what people want to know is simply to ask them. Conduct a survey to find out how much they already know about the subject, what they'd most like to know, and where they'd go for more information. You should get some very useful responses that could form the basis of your book. You might make some useful contacts too. Don't give up the survey if some people aren't interested and walk away. Just like writing, the secret of success is to be persistent.

FAQs

As I mentioned earlier, FAQs (Frequently Asked Questions) make a fantastic starting point when you're planning your book. Again, you'll need to rewrite the questions and answers in your own words. You can find FAQs on the internet, especially in newsgroups and discussion forums.

Getting lively

While you're looking through newsgroups and discussion forums, look for interesting questions that aren't covered in the FAQs. You might also find recommendations of particular products, details of new websites, anecdotes, book reviews, and more. Anecdotes are a particularly useful way of livening up your book. If you come across a good one, email the person and ask for permission to use it in your book.

Learning by doing

I've likened writing a non-fiction book to teaching a class on the subject. This reminds me of when I first started teaching IT (Information Technology). It wasn't long before I started getting complaints. My classes mainly consisted of me demonstrating the features of each product. But my students didn't want to just watch me; they wanted to have a go too. I quickly changed the format so that as I demonstrated each feature I gave them the opportunity to try it for themselves. The classes became a great success. Unfortunately it now took twice as long to cover the material. But at least they were happy.

These students will have retained their knowledge much better by getting involved than if they'd simply watched me do everything. So it makes sense to make your book as much of a hands-on experience as possible. Give them exercises or experiments to do and let them get their hands dirty. You could also provide them with your contact details, or set up a website with a discussion forum so they can ask for extra guidance if something goes horribly wrong.

> When readers tell you that an exercise or experiment went wrong, it's valuable feedback. When you write your next book, or a revised edition of the current one, you can discuss the problems they encountered, explain why they occurred, and show ways of solving them.

Structure

The way you organise your facts can make all the difference between a successful book and a useless one – or a published one and an unpublishable one. Try organising your facts into different structures. Do they flow logically and smoothly from one point to the next? If not then you might have used the wrong structure, you might have a section missing, or you might need to add a few more facts to plug the gaps.

Have you grouped your facts into similar topics, or are they scattered randomly throughout the book? If there's no logical grouping then it's almost impossible for readers to look up a fact quickly. Remember, the emphasis is on *adding value*.

Finding the best structure

The most obvious structure might not be the best one. Just because all the other books do it that way doesn't mean you have to too, especially if you want your book to stand out. However, if you've studied the other books and decided that their structure really is the best, then you should use it too.

Quick – you're in charge!

Imagine that an evening class teacher has dropped out at the last minute. The organiser knows you're something of an expert in the subject and persuades you to step in. You now have to prepare fifteen or twenty lesson plans, each lasting two hours, aiming to cover the entire subject at whatever level the students are currently studying. It'll take you quite a while to work out those lesson plans, but when they're done you'll have the complete structure of your book: each lesson plan becomes a chapter.

Knowing where to begin

Try to organise your book so you start giving information straight away. If your readers discover that they've immediately learnt something new, they'll know they're going to get great value from the rest of the book.

Many non-fiction books begin with a history of the subject. However, unless it's a vital part of the book it's important not to dwell on the historical aspect for too long. If the information is available elsewhere, give a quick overview and then refer your readers to your book's bibliography section. You don't need to mention the historical aspect at all if you're aiming your book at intermediate and advanced levels. You can safely assume that your readers already know that part.

Question and answer format

This makes a good way of structuring a book, especially if you've already collected sample questions and answers from magazines and the internet as we discussed earlier. Divide them into groups of related topics to form chapters. Each chapter could then consist of a paragraph or two of introduction, followed by a number of related questions and answers, each with an appropriate heading or sub-heading.

Can't write a book? Think again!

You don't need to be able to write or type to write a non-fiction book – just talk. Design your book's structure as above, then divide it into chapters. Take one of those chapters and immerse yourself in that topic for a whole day. At the end of the day, stand up and give a thirty-minute speech on it. Have a tape recorder running while you do this.

Use a lapel microphone rather than the recorder's built-in microphone when you give speeches. The sound quality will be much better, making it easier to transcribe the recording into text.

Don't read from notes; speak directly from your head and your heart. If you've spent the day well, researching the subject and preparing as if you were going to give a real presentation, then you should have plenty of material to fill the time, and be able to cover every point in sufficient detail. Remember to entertain your audience as well as educate them, so if you've picked up a few anecdotes or jokes, slip them in too.

All you have to do now is rewind the tape and type it up – or get someone else to do it for you. That's an entire chapter finished in one day!

If you already give speeches, then you've already done the hard work of planning, organising, structuring and writing. Why not compile a collection of your speeches in book form? This will enhance your reputation as an expert *and* as a published author. You'll also be able to sell copies of your book whenever you give one of your talks.

Perhaps your after-dinner speeches have earned you recognition. Again, a collection of these speeches in book form could do very well and will be quick to write.

If you don't give speeches yourself but you know someone who does, see if you can persuade him to work with you on a book. All you have to do is wire him up with a lapel microphone plugged into a small cassette recorder or digital voice recorder in his pocket each time he gives one of his speeches. Afterwards, type up the speech and edit it as necessary. When you have enough, sort the transcripts into logical order, write an introduction, and the book's finished.

You'll need to come to an arrangement about how to split the profits. The speaker makes extra money from his talks for absolutely no effort whatsoever – all he did was wear a microphone during speeches that he would have given anyway. And you too will have made money for very little effort – just a bit of organising and typing. You'd be fools to let an opportunity like this slip by.

Becoming more marketable

It always pays to get your name around if you're writing a book. If you haven't written any magazine articles yet, now would be a good time to do it. When these are published, you'll instantly gain expert status. If your book has already been published, make sure the magazine mentions your book at the end of each article. That'll boost your credibility even higher – and it's a great advert for the book. Writing these articles needn't involve much work; they can be simple extracts from your book or condensed versions of some of the chapters. If people want to read the full versions, then they'll just have to buy your book!

If you're trying to get a publisher to accept your proposal, showing him copies of your published magazine articles will significantly increase your chances of success.

Boosting your credibility

If you look at the author profiles in non-fiction books, you'll often find that they've taught the subject at some point in their careers. You need to bring yourself up to their level of credibility.

Could you run an evening class or something like that, even if it's just for a couple of weeks? You can then claim with complete honesty that you've taught the subject. Most local colleges publish spring and autumn schedules of evening classes. Get in touch with the organisers and see if you can get yourself added to the next schedule. You'll have to prove you're an expert of course, and draw up a set of lesson plans.

The book of the course

If your book is based on a course you teach, your aim should be that by the end of the book and by the end of the course both groups should be equally knowledgeable. There will be some differences of course. If you write the book after you've finished teaching the class, you'll know what worked and what didn't and be able to correct any mistakes. You might also be able to go into much more detail than you had time for in class.

Those who attended your classes will probably have had more hands-on experience. Try to replicate as much of this as possible in your book by including exercises and experiments for your readers to carry out. Your book might also include examples of work the students produced in class, perhaps with photographs of what they achieved. You could also take photos of your students in action and use these in your book. Make sure you get each student's permission to use their photo.

Writing with authority

Tone of voice and writing style are very important when writing non-fiction. You need to write with authority and sound like an expert. Think about the best speech or presentation you've ever heard. Could you do it as well as that? If not, why not? It's the sort of level you *should* be aiming for.

A great speaker's expertise is self-evident. He knows the subject inside out and backwards. You can ask him any question and he not only knows the answer but could talk about it at length (or so it seems). He speaks confidently, clearly, and loud enough to be heard at the back. He doesn't rely on notes. He can tailor the length of his talk from a couple of minutes to a couple of hours at a moment's notice. He has absolute conviction in what he's saying. The audience sits up and listens, enthralled and excited, and leaves the room feeling exhilarated, inspired, motivated and entertained. That's what you should be trying to emulate in your book.

Dr Dave's Writing Revolution

How about coming up with a new technique and putting your own name on it? You're setting up your own little niche in the market – with no competition. You'll get to do all the TV, radio, newspaper and magazine interviews you want. You could travel from city to city or country to country, giving workshops and lectures – and selling lots of books along the way. You're putting your expertise, reputation and authority right up front where everyone can see it. You're using your name as a brand and a marketing tool.

For a great example, look at Dr Atkins' New Diet Revolution. Dr Atkins made a lot of money, sold millions of books, and was never out of the news thanks to the storm of controversy his technique generated. If you ask people to name a diet, his will be the one most people think of first.

Magazine articles

The techniques in this book can also be used to write magazine articles very quickly. Again, send a query letter to start with and don't write the article until it's been accepted. On average, one in twelve queries is accepted, so if you send out fifty queries in a month, you should expect only four to succeed. Because you'll need to send out large numbers of queries, it's a good idea to set up a template in your word processor with most of the details already completed.

Always send queries by post unless you've established a working relationship with the editor and he's agreed to accept them by email. Always enclose an SAE. And always address queries to a named person, never 'The Editor'.

The next step

In the next chapter we'll look at some modern technologies and clever techniques that can multiply your productivity many times over.

13   You have the technology

You might be wondering how long it actually takes to type your book. Let's look at some numbers. A typical novel is around 80,000 words, so we'll use that as our guideline. A reasonable typing speed is around 40 words per minute (wpm). At that speed, it'll take 2,000 minutes (33 hours) to type your book, so you'll need to type for just over an hour a day to finish it in a month. That doesn't mean a solid hour of typing though. You could split it into several fifteen-minute sessions.

What if you increased your speed to 100 wpm? Now your book will only take 800 minutes (13 hours) to type – twenty-five minutes a day.

In this chapter, we'll look at how to get your words onto paper at the rate of one hundred words per minute or faster. It's possible to do that just by learning to type faster, so let's look at that first and then we'll consider some other options.

We'll also look at some tools and techniques to make writing your book easier. They won't necessarily make you write any faster, but ease counts for a lot too.

Typing faster

There are several typing tutorials available, both in book form and as computer programs. The one I use and recommend is Mavis Beacon Teaches Typing. It's suitable for everyone, from children to adults and from complete beginners to experienced typists. Its aim is to make everyone who uses it type like a professional.

Figure 13.1 Mavis Beacon Teaches Typing 15

The program adjusts itself to suit you. If you're a complete beginner, it starts by showing you how to sit correctly and position your hands on the keyboard. Then it takes you through all the keys in easy stages. On-screen hands show you which fingers to use to press each key. If you're more experienced, you can skip that part and do a typing test to discover your current speed. Then you can set yourself a goal; a twenty-five percent speed increase is a good goal to begin with.

If you practise for fifteen minutes a day, your typing speed should increase by twenty-five percent in two weeks. With further practise, you could eventually reach speeds of over 120 wpm.

The program includes several different types of lesson, each carefully designed to increase your speed and accuracy. You can let the program decide which path to take through the lessons, or you can design your own customised lessons.

There are several games too – the faster and more accurately you type, the better your score will be. In the car race, for example, you have to type faster to get ahead of the other cars and win.

The program monitors everything you type and shows your overall speed, your accuracy, and your actual speed taking into account the errors. It also shows you which keys you have the most trouble with, and automatically designs special lessons so you can practise those keys more thoroughly.

The latest version features audio exercises, so you can practice typing from dictation. It also supports the Microsoft Natural Keyboard as well as standard keyboards.

Dvorak keyboard layout

It's a common misperception that the standard QWERTY keyboard layout was designed to slow typists down. That was never the intention. It did slow them down a little – not, as many people think, because the brain can't remember where the keys are, but

> QWERTY was designed to prevent adjacent keys from jamming on manual type-writers. It separates the most common letter pairs.

because the fingers have to stretch further to reach the most commonly used letters.

There's really no need for the QWERTY layout now, but we've stuck with it anyway. We could have switched back to ABC. But if we're going to change the layout, is there an even better way of laying out the keys that avoids all that stretching?

Dr August Dvorak's layout puts the most commonly used letters on the middle row, with the strongest fingers used to hit the most common keys.

Figure 13.2 Dvorak keyboard layout

If I type *ideas4writers* using a QWERTY keyboard, only three letters are on the middle row: A, S and D. I'll have to stretch my fingers nine times to reach the other letters and one number. But if I type it with a Dvorak keyboard, I only need to stretch to reach the 4, R and W keys. Everything else is right under my fingers on the middle row. It really does work!

The Dvorak layout won't necessarily make you type any faster, but it will reduce the amount of stretching you have to do. This minimises the risk of repetitive strain injury (RSI).

The general consensus among Dvorak devotees is that it's about twelve percent faster than QWERTY – and significantly more comfortable.

Dvorak keyboards are available to buy, but they're expensive and hard to find. Fortunately, you can easily switch to the Dvorak layout and continue using existing keyboard. You just need to change a setting in the Windows Control Panel. Set the keyboard layout to 'United States – Dvorak' or 'US English – Dvorak'.

Your keyboard now speaks Dvorak – which means you'll have to learn to touch-type because the letters on the keys won't match what appears on the screen. Some people paint over the keys with nail varnish to blank them out. Alternatively, you could put stickers on the keys to show the new layout. It's also a good idea to stick a Dvorak layout diagram to your monitor to help you learn to type without looking at the keys – you'll learn it much faster that way.

Shorthand typing

Another way of speeding up the writing process is to use shorthand. Most versions use squiggly marks to represent words and sounds, but that won't help you to type any faster. It's also useless if you're trying to persuade someone else to type up your notes for you.

A better method is to drop vowels and unnecessary letters: T ct st o t mt (The cat sat on the mat). The advantage of this method is that you only have to type half the number of characters, so you can (in theory) type twice as fast. However, you'll probably have to stop and think about how to abbreviate some words, which will slow you down. A good solution in that case is to simply write the word in full.

> If you decide to type abbreviated words in your word processor, turn off the spell checker.

EasyScript and ComputerScript

EasyScript is very much as I described above – you leave out non-essential vowels and letters. But it adds five simple rules, so everyone who uses it abbreviates words in the same way. There are several advantages:

> Here's some text written in EasyScript:
> H fstr u tpe, h qckr u wl expc suc. (35 key presses)
> And the full version:
> The faster you type, the quicker you will experience success. (61 key presses)

- You can use EasyScript whether you're writing by hand or typing

- It's easier to learn than other forms of shorthand

- Most people can read what you've written, even if they don't know EasyScript.

- You can expand EasyScript into full text automatically using ComputerScript

Create your own version of ComputerScript in Microsoft Word by entering abbreviations into the AutoCorrect table. For a gentle start, use the following single letter abbreviations. b: be, c: see, d: and, f: if, h: the, q: queue, r: are, s: is, t: it, u: you, w: we, y: why.

There are three levels of EasyScript. Level 1 aims to get you writing at 40 wpm. Level 2 takes you up to 80 wpm. Level 3 goes up to 130 wpm. Each level can be purchased separately, with or without ComputerScript.

Reaching the highest speeds will take considerable practice, but it's worth persevering because, like learning to type, you'll reap the benefits for the rest of your writing career.

IntelliEdit and IntelliComplete

Here's another way of reducing the amount of typing you need to do. IntelliEdit can be downloaded from FlashPeak Software's website (www.flashpeak.com). It's a text editor that runs in any version of Microsoft Windows. It looks perfectly normal until you type the first couple of characters, but then something interesting happens...

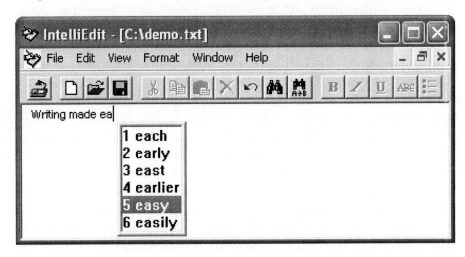

Figure 13.3 IntelliEdit

As you start typing, a pop-up box appears with a list of words beginning with those characters. If the word you want is on the list, press the number key that corresponds to its position in the list and

IntelliEdit inserts it into your document. If the word isn't on the list, type the next character or two and the list updates itself. When the right word appears, press its number.

As you type, the words you use most frequently move to the top of the list, so you'll find yourself typing fewer and fewer characters.

> To type *Writing made easy* in full requires 17 key presses. Using IntelliEdit, I typed *Wr4 m1 ea5*, which is only 10 key presses. It's virtually impossible to make spelling mistakes, so children and dyslexics should find it useful too.

IntelliComplete works in exactly the same way, but rather than being a separate text editor, it adds the IntelliEdit function to any Windows application – such as Microsoft Word or whichever word processor you use.

IntelliEdit is free. IntelliComplete costs $49.97 (approx £26.50). I recommend trying the free version first to see how well you get on with it.

AutoText

If you use Microsoft Word, AutoText allows you to store frequently used phrases and type them with just a few keystrokes.

Type a phrase such as *It was a dark and stormy night.* Highlight it with your mouse, then click on the Tools menu and choose Auto-Correct. Click on the AutoText tab. The phrase you typed is shown in the preview window and in the box labelled 'Enter AutoText entry here'. You can leave the text in the box alone, or replace it with something shorter and more memorable, such as *dsnight*. Let's leave it alone for now. Click the Add button, then click OK.

Start a new paragraph and begin typing the same phrase. After a few characters, a yellow box appears showing the full phrase. Press Enter to accept it, and the full phrase appears in your document.

AutoText is useful for storing things you type frequently, such as your name and address, greetings and sign-off phrases (Dear Sir, yours sincerely), standard phrases (Thank you for your letter), copy-right information, details of previously published work, a potted biography for query letters, standard answers to frequently asked questions, and so on. The more you use it, the more uses you'll think of – and the more time you'll save.

Stenography, Palantype and Machine Shorthand

For the sake of completeness, I've investigated using these systems to write your book. Proficient users can type well over 200 wpm and easily keep up with real-time speech.

To use the system you press several keys simultaneously, forming a chord. Each chord represents a syllable, a word, or a common phrase. The machines are usually connected to a separate computer or laptop, which translates the chord patterns into normal text.

Figure 13.4 Stenograph machine

Unfortunately, the machines are very expensive – about the same as a high-end laptop in the case of the latest Stenograph machines. The software is very expensive too. And then you have to take into account the considerable amount of training required. According to one instructor, mastering the basics takes about a year, and to become fully proficient takes two years. Students are expected to practice for at least four hours every day during that time, and the training course costs around £3000.

If you're a court reporter, or if you already use one of these machines in your job, then you should be able to use this equipment to write your book very quickly indeed. If not, then it's not really worth pursuing this option.

Writing on the move

With a portable word processor, you can work in the garden, on the beach, or wherever you like. You could also write anywhere using a notepad, or by dictating your text into a voice recorder, but I prefer to use a word processor.

You might immediately think of using a laptop computer. Unfortunately, they're not as convenient as I'd like them to be. They're heavy, expensive, slow to start up, and the battery usually only lasts for a couple of hours.

So my choice is the AlphaSmart Dana. It's smaller and lighter than a laptop, but has a full-size keyboard and a large clear screen (with backlight) which displays about eleven lines of text. It starts up instantly – press the 'on' button and start typing. It's simple to connect to your main computer to transfer files. And the battery lasts for twenty hours.

Figure 13.5 AlphaSmart Dana

For more details visit AlphaSmart's website – www.alphasmart.co.uk

If you're interested in buying one, I can recommend TAG Learning (www.taglearning.co.uk). Don't do what I did and try to order one direct from AlphaSmart, as they aren't really geared up to handle sales in the UK. The Dana costs around £325 including VAT.

For noting down ideas, I use a Psion Revo. This is a pocket computer with a built-in word processor, spreadsheet, address book, jotter, and all sorts of other useful tools. The jotter is my favourite, and makes it very easy to organise your ideas. The keyboard is small but usable, though you wouldn't want to write a book on it. I wouldn't be without mine.

Unfortunately, Psion have stopped making them and there's no real equivalent on the market at the moment. Fortunately, there are always plenty of second-hand ones for sale on eBay (www.ebay.co.uk)

Figure 13.6 Psion Revo

Say it out loud

Normal speech can be well over 200 wpm, but you'll probably speak more slowly when dictating your book. My dictation speed is 158 wpm, but that's still three times faster than I can type.

Some people have problems with dictating. The secret, which I mentioned earlier, is to break down the writing into small chunks. Spend a few minutes considering each chunk before writing or saying a single word. That way you won't dry up mid-sentence, or struggle for the right word.

I recommend finding someone else to type up your dictation for you – preferably someone who can type a lot faster than you. There's nothing more tedious than trying to type up your own words from tape, especially if you're eager to get started on the next section of your book. It might even be worth paying a professional audio typist to transcribe your tapes for you. When you start earning money from all those books you're going to write, a typing service will pay for itself many times over. You really will be able to write your book as fast as you can speak.

How long it would take to write your book if you could type at 200 wpm? 80,000 words at 200 wpm is 400 minutes (six and a half hours). You could write the whole book in a single day!

It's important to speak very clearly when you dictate onto tape. It's far better to slow down a little than to discover you can't make out half the words when you play the tape back. Spend some time practising dictating and playing back the tape to get a feel for the best speed, how loudly or quietly you should speak, how close you need to be to the microphone, and so on.

Choosing voice recording equipment

There are several different types of voice recorders, and all have advantages and disadvantages.

Dictaphones

Many audio typists use foot-operated mini cassette players. This allows them to scroll backwards and forwards through the tape without removing their hands from the keyboard. If that's what your typist uses, then you'll need compatible equipment – a pocket cassette recorder or Dictaphone. Make sure yours uses the same tapes as your typist, and get plenty of spare tapes because they only hold twenty minutes per side and your typist will be typing up one set while you record another. Number the tapes so the typist knows which order they go in.

Pocket cassette recorders are widely available and affordable. Their built-in microphones are convenient, but they pick up other sounds, including noise from the machines themselves, so the quality is average to poor. For normal dictation though, these machines are perfectly adequate.

Pros: Affordable, portable, widely available, compatible with most audio typists' equipment.

Cons: Average/poor sound quality, tapes only hold twenty minutes per side.

MiniDisc

If you want high quality recordings, I recommend using a MiniDisc recorder coupled with a decent microphone. Standard MiniDiscs hold up to an hour of near-CD quality stereo sound. But here's a sneaky trick: most MiniDisc recorders also have a mono mode, so you can double the storage time to two hours per disc. You can also get HD MiniDiscs, which have a much great capacity, but you'll need a compatible recorder to use them.

Because of their high quality and easy portability, MiniDiscs are widely used by radio journalists for recording interviews for broadcast.

Pros: High quality sound, portability, long recording time, can also be used for music.

Cons: Cost of recorders, audio typists probably won't be able to use them.

Cassette recorders

Another option for home or office-based recording is to use an ordinary cassette recorder. These are available quite cheaply and use standard cassette tapes. For optimum quality, use a good quality external microphone rather than the built-in one – check whether your recorder has a microphone socket.

Pros: Widely available, affordable, long recording time, good sound quality.

Cons: Audio typists might not be able to use these tapes.

Digital voice recorders

Digital voice recorders are becoming increasingly common, and many are so small you can pop them into your shirt pocket and forget they're there. You'd expect something labelled 'digital' to have excellent sound quality. Unfortunately, this isn't always the case, especially with the cheaper models. They use very high compression to squeeze as much recording time as possible into a small amount of memory. The result is poor sound quality – though you do usually get long recording times. Mine can store four hours in 'high quality' mode.

Better models can take external memory cards, have variable compression settings, and allow you to transfer the sound files to your computer for long-term storage and playback.

As I mentioned earlier, once you've copied the sound files to your computer, you could use dictation software to transcribe the files automatically and save the cost of hiring a typist. You'll need to make sure the sound quality is good enough though.

Pros: Small, no moving parts, non-sequential file storage, can transfer files to computer for automatic transcription (some models only).

Cons: Poor sound quality on some models, good ones are expensive.

Emergency measures

As I mentioned earlier, if you have an idea that's too good to risk losing, you could phone home and dictate it onto your answering machine. Or phone a friend and ask him to write it down. Or do what I do and use your mobile phone to write yourself a text message.

Dictation Software

You could dictate your book straight into your computer using software such as Dragon NaturallySpeaking, mentioned above. There are several versions of NaturallySpeaking, and the more you pay, the more features you get. The Preferred edition, for example, includes a microphone and RealSpeak, which reads your text back to you. The Mobile edition includes a good quality digital voice recorder. Other dictation software is available, including IBM ViaVoice.

Keyboards

A decent keyboard is essential for fast typing. You'll spend a lot of time pounding those keys, so you need to be comfortable. Unfortunately, some manufacturers' idea of a quality keyboard is one where you have to hit the keys with considerable force. After a while your wrists ache. So it's worth shopping around and trying out several different keyboards to find one that suits you. It needs to be adjustable to the correct angle, and have just the right amount of softness, firmness, springiness or clickiness to suit your typing style.

I now use a Microsoft Natural Keyboard, which is angled to fit the curve of your wrist and the shape of your hand. The result is a far more comfortable typing position, though it takes some getting used to.

I have a test you should try. Let your arms go limp and your hands and wrists go floppy, then place them on your keyboard with your thumbs on the spacebar and your index fingers on the F and J keys. Let your other fingers fall naturally wherever they like, with no tension or twisting. Which keys are your fingers on? Probably not the 'official' typing keys: A S D F for the left hand, and J K L ; for the right hand.

My left fingers are on Q W E F, and my right fingers are on J I O P. Now put your fingers on the 'official' keys (the middle row) and you'll notice that you need to bend your wrists inwards quite a long way. When I did that test at the end of last year, I immediately went out and bought a Natural keyboard.

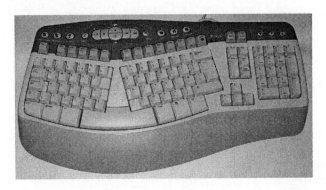

Figure 13.7 Microsoft Natural Keyboard

Other writing software

There are several story-writing packages available that will help make your life easier. Not only do they make the writing process faster, but they guide you through each step of the story, ensuring that it's complete and well told. I've tested and reviewed several of these packages on the ideas4writers.co.uk website. The ones I liked best were StoryCraft Pro, StoryWeaver, and WriteItNow.

StoryCraft Pro

StoryCraft Pro is my personal favourite out of all the packages I've reviewed. It's a complete writing course that holds your hand at every stage as you write. You can use it to write short stories and scripts as well as novels. Beginners will find it very useful and will keep using it time and time again. More experienced writers can use it to put together the outline of a great story very quickly, and find and fix problems in stories that aren't working.

Like many of the other story-writing programs available, Story-Craft Pro is based on Christopher Vogler's book *The Writer's Journey*, and Joseph Campbell's *The Hero with a Thousand Faces*, which both cover the structure of heroic myths that we looked at in Chapter 11.

StoryCraft Pro is extremely easy to use, and it only takes a few minutes to become completely familiar with the way it works. There's a vast amount of help contained in the tutorial section, which guides you as you move from step to step.

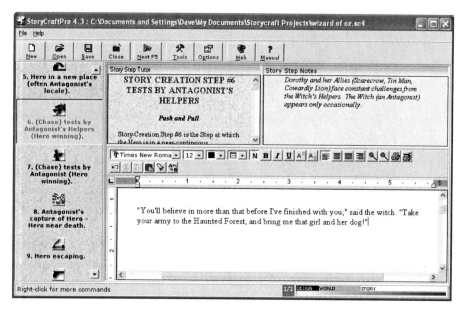

Figure 13.8 StoryCraft Pro

You start by designing the basic structure of your story. First you have to decide on the concept, such as 'love of money brings about downfall'. Then you have to decide which category of story you're writing: plot-based, character-based or epic. Next you choose the story type, which includes chase, puzzle, revenge and several others. Finally you need to design the 'world' (the location or environment where your story takes place) and the characters.

Once you've entered the basic details, StoryCraft Pro analyses your story and matches it against one of the eighteen basic patterns that have been used in myths through the ages. That pattern is then broken down into twelve fundamental steps for you to follow as you write the story.

As you go through each step and read the accompanying tutorial, you'll start to have ideas about your story, which you can add to the notes box. When you're ready to start writing, you can use the built-in word processor to start fleshing out your notes. The tutorial and notes remain on the screen throughout the writing process for easy reference. The plot and story structure update continuously as you write, and they can be viewed as an outline or printed at any time.

StoryCraft Pro costs $79 (approx £41.95) from the StoryCraft Pro website (www.storycraftpro.com). Full details, screenshots, and an online walkthrough are also available on their website.

StoryWeaver

StoryWeaver consists of a set of 'cards', each containing questions, suggestions, ideas and information about the story you're writing. There are around 200 cards, split into various categories which are listed down the left side of the screen.

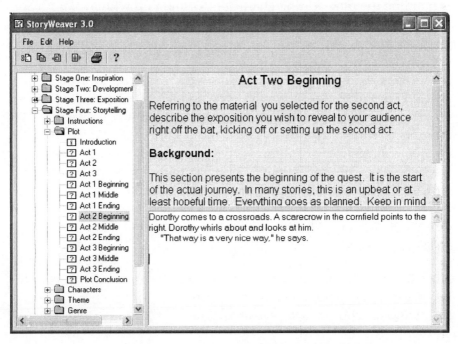

Figure 13.9 StoryWeaver 3.0

The main categories are:

- Inspiration
- Development
- Exposition
- Storytelling

Each of these is further subdivided into:

- Plot
- Characters
- Theme
- Genre

If you follow the cards in order, they start by getting you to come up with a plot idea. Their suggestion is to combine three random words and make up a story using them. If you already have a plot in mind, or if you'd prefer to use a different technique for generating ideas, then you can use that. It then takes you through the process of expanding the plot, adding characters, coming up with problems and issues to be overcome, and so on. Then you move on to the next category and go on expanding and developing your story. It's very comprehensive.

Each card is very clear, with a simple explanation of what you need to do, some questions to answer, and suggestions and examples on how to proceed. They're far more comprehensive and wide-ranging than you first suspect, and the result – which is what really counts – should be excellent, even for novice writers. If you work through all of the cards, you'll end up with a well-rounded story structure with no holes in the plot and no weak characters.

I've tested the program thoroughly, and I'm confident that it will always produce a solid outline that you could develop into a great story.

StoryWeaver 3.0 costs $29.95 (approx £15.90) from Storymind (www.storymind.com). You'll find more details, screenshots, and a free demo version on their website.

WriteItNow

WriteItNow is a little different, because it doesn't guide you through the story-writing process. Instead, it acts as a combined word processor, database, organiser, and idea-generating package, aimed specifically at novelists.

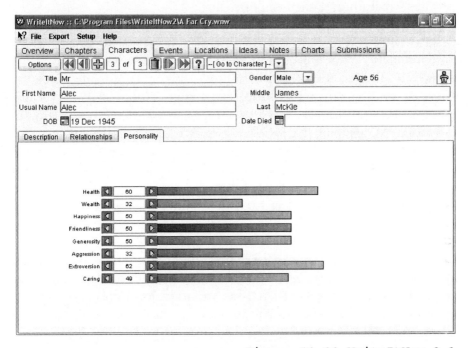

Figure 13.10 WriteItNow 2.1

Click on the first tab for an overview of your novel. The second tab is where you store your chapters as you write them. Other tabs store the characters, locations, events, and notes. The chart tab shows the relationships between the characters. There's also a timeline of the key events.

The Submissions tab records where and when you submitted work for publication, the result (accepted or rejected), the publication date, the amount received, and so on. You could use this to record information about everything you write, not just novels.

The word processor is basic, but enough to get by, and there's a built-in spell checker. It can also display statistical information such as the number of words and the readability – the reading age a person would need in order to understand what you've written.

WriteItNow is a modern way of storing all the notes for your novel in one place, rather than having hundreds of pieces of paper scattered everywhere – some of which you'll never be able to find again.

Two important components of the system are the character generator and the idea generator. You can generate complete character profiles – including names – in one click.

A basic storyline comes together very quickly, even if you have no idea what you want to write about. Start by generating a character automatically. When I tried it, it came up with a chap called Andrew Patterson. It also generated Andrew's attributes (health, wealth, strength, and so on), which you can change if you want to. It also mentioned his childhood friend, Ashley McNamara. That's useful – I immediately created another character. It told me that Andrew had been married for ten years to a girl named Stephanie Logan, so I created another character based on her. It also told me the date of their marriage and plotted it on the timeline.

With three characters created in a matter of seconds, I used the idea generator to come up with a storyline in one click. In this case: *Andrew thinks Ashley has stolen something from him*. I made a note of that in the Notes section. You can carry on generating more ideas like this, and noting down all the good ones, until the rough outline of a story begins to emerge. You can then think about the locations, and create a record for each place. Then you can organise the story into events and group them into chapters.

There are several free add-ons available on the WriteItNow website, providing timelines and background information for periods such as Victorian Britain, Tudor Britain, Stuart Britain, and so on. If you enter your character's date of birth, the program provides you with a list of historic events that took place within their lifetime. It even tells you how old they would have been when that event occurred. The add-ons can also generate authentic names from that period and provide other background material about day-to-day life.

WriteItNow 2 costs £19.95 from Ravenshead Services (www.ravensheadservices.com). Full details, screenshots, and a free demo version are also available on their website.

WriteItNow 2 is also sold under the name Write Your Own Novel – Professional, and is widely available from computer stores and on-line retailers such as Amazon.

Final Draft

I'd just like to give a quick mention to a program called Final Draft. This software is for scriptwriters and screenwriters, so if you want to write films, TV shows or plays, then it's just what you need – just about everyone who's anyone in Hollywood uses it. Go to the Final Draft website (www.finaldraft.com) for full details. There's a fantastic online walk-through – just sit back and watch the show as it takes you through the whole product.

Writing longhand

Although I've concentrated on using a word processor for the majority of this book, many writers prefer to write everything by hand. So here are a few tips for them.

Make sure your writing is legible. Somebody – perhaps even you – will have to read it at some point in order to type it into a word processor. The more difficult your writing is to read, the longer it'll take to type. So it pays to slow down a little and take more care if you have to. You'll save time (and perhaps money) in the end.

Another useful tip, unless you're writing in small notebooks, is to divide each page of your writing pad into two columns. Draw a line down the middle of the page, then write from top to bottom down the left-hand column. When you reach the bottom, write from top to bottom down the right-hand column. This significantly reduces the arm and wrist movements you have to make across the page, so it's less tiring and slightly faster.

I mentioned a shorthand system called EasyScript earlier in the chapter. You can use this system when writing longhand as well as typing. You only have to write half the number of characters in each word, so you can write much faster. EasyScript gives you a simple set of rules to follow when abbreviating each word, so you don't have to stop and think about how to write it. The other advantage is that it's still fairly readable, so you could get someone else to type it up for you even if they haven't learnt EasyScript themselves.

There are other forms of shorthand, such as Pitman's. However, these are far more difficult to learn since they involve drawing squiggly lines to represent words and sounds. You can't just hand your notepad over to someone else and get them to type it up for you unless they understand shorthand too.

Microsoft Word

Microsoft Word is the most popular word processor in the world and can save you vast amounts of time. There isn't room for a complete Word course in this book, but I'd like to point out some of the features that will save you time or make your life easier.

Spell checker

Word underlines incorrect and questionable spellings in red as you type. I recommend turning this function off while you're writing, as it's too distracting. Stopping to correct every mistake will interrupt your flow. Turn it back on again when you come to edit your work. To correct a mistake, right-click on the underlined word and a list of suggested corrections appears. If the correct spelling is there, click it and it's fixed.

Grammar checker

There's also an automatic grammar checker, but most people keep this turned off, as it's not particularly reliable. There's no harm in turning it on when you edit your work though, as it might pick up a few mistakes you missed. Word underlines grammar mistakes in green. Right-click on these to find out why they're wrong, or to see a suggested version.

Thesaurus

When you're searching for just the right word, or looking for another way of saying something, a thesaurus comes in handy. Word has one built-in. In the most recent versions you can simply right-click on any word, click on 'synonyms' and it displays a list of alternatives. If you see one you like, click it and it immediately replaces that word in your text.

Headers and footers

The headers and footers tool is a boon for book writers. It automatically puts certain pieces of information at the top and bottom of every page: your name, the book title, the chapter number and name, the page number, and so on. This saves at least one line of typing on every page. If you decide to change anything in the header or footer, you only have to do it once and all the other pages update automatically.

Templates
If you find yourself writing the same letters time after time, a template can save you time. Set up a template for your query letters for example, and you only need to enter the name and address of the editor on each letter. Everything else – your name and address, a description of your book, your marketing plan, your publishing history and personal details – is already there.

Find and Replace
Every word processor has this essential function, though Word's is more sophisticated than most. If you decide to change a character's name, for example, you just need to enter his old name and his new name and click 'Replace All'. The more advanced find and replace features let you replace all word forms. For example, if you wanted to replace *help* with *assist* it would also replace *helped* with *assisted*, *helping* with *assisting* and so on. You can also replace formatting, so you could instruct it to replace all italics with underlines.

Outliner
Word has an excellent built-in outliner, which you can use to plan and organise the structure of your book. See Chapter 7 for full details.

Keyboard shortcuts and bookmarks
Use keyboard shortcuts to zoom around even the largest documents in a fraction of a second, rather than scrolling laboriously with your mouse. You can also apply formatting and use other commands using keyboard shortcuts instead of the toolbars and menus. The shortcuts are listed in Word's online help: Press the F1 key, then find the section called *Using keyboard shortcuts*.

Table of Contents and Index
Word can generate the table of contents automatically, based on the headings and sub-headings you used. If you move things around and the page numbers change, just generate the table of contents again; it only takes a few seconds. It can also generate an index for you. All you have to do is go through the text and mark the words you'd like it to include. Again, if you move things around later, it doesn't matter; just update the index.

It's important to bear in mind that when books are published, the number of words per page will be different from your Word document. The table of contents and index you produced in Word will no longer be correct. However, with your Word-generated version to hand, all you have to do is go through the publisher's proofs and enter the correct page numbers. It's a terrific time saver.

Customisable toolbars

It's easy to customise Word's toolbars to remove the buttons you never use and add the functions you really need. Just right-click on a toolbar and choose Customise. To remove a button from the toolbar, drag it off the toolbar and release the mouse. To add a new function, choose the one you want from the list of commands and drag it onto the toolbar. If you don't like the default button, you can easily change it.

In my copy of Word, I've added new buttons to switch between single-spacing and double-spacing, print the current page only, and display the word count.

Macros

If Word doesn't have the function you need, then you can create your own. At the most basic level, that simply means recording the steps you took to achieve something and then playing them back at the click of a button.

I've added a macro that automatically pastes plain text when I click a button on the toolbar. This is especially useful if I copy some text from a web page and don't want to retain the formatting, links, table layouts and so on. I simply recorded the steps to do this – Edit menu, Paste Special, Unformatted Text, OK – as a macro, then added it to the toolbar as a new button.

There's also a built-in programming language, so you can create much more complex functions than this. Fortunately, it's unlikely you'll need to do this when you're writing a book.

AutoCorrect

The AutoCorrect function fixes most typing errors automatically – you might not even notice that it's done it. If you type *adn*, for example, it'll change it to *and* all by itself. If you regularly misspell certain words, add the incorrect spelling and the correct spelling to the AutoCorrect table and it'll fix it automatically next time you make that mistake.

AutoText

AutoText enters whole chunks of text at once. If a word or phrase is stored in the AutoText table, it appears in a yellow box as soon as you type the first few characters. Press the Enter key to paste it into your document.

Master documents

If you've stored each chapter of your book as a separate Word document, a master document allows you to treat the whole book as a single unit. For example, the page numbers will run continuously from the first page in chapter one to the last page in the final chapter, rather than restarting from one at the beginning of each new chapter. Master documents are also useful when you generate automatic tables of contents or indexes.

Mail merge

When you're sending out the same letter to several different people, you don't want to keep retyping it, especially if they're people you write to regularly. The mail merge function allows you to store everyone's name, address and other details in a database, and automatically insert them in the right place on each copy of the document. This could be just the thing you need if you regularly send out query letters to publishers and agents, or if you write to existing customers to tell them about your new book. You can get Word to print the envelopes and address labels for you too.

A cheaper way of getting Microsoft Word

It's all very well going on about Microsoft Word, you might be thinking, but it's a very expensive program and I can't really afford it. So here's a way to get it for a fraction of the normal retail price. Buy *Microsoft Works Suite* – make sure you get the Suite version, not the standard version. This includes a number of very useful applications, aimed at home office users rather than large businesses. The different market is reflected in the much lower price. The word processor in Works Suite is the full version of Word.

By the way, Works Suite 2004 and Works Suite 2005 both contain the same version of Word. You can therefore make an even bigger saving by buying the 2004 version, as it's being sold off cheaply. The New and Used Marketplace on Amazon (www.amazon.co.uk) is a good place to look. At the time of writing, a brand new copy of Works Suite 2004 is available for just £24.99.

ideas4writers.co.uk

In the back of this book you'll find a voucher for three months free membership of ideas4writers.co.uk – the ideas and inspiration website. As well as the thousands of ideas available to members, there are several writing engines. These are online programs that automatically generate characters and storylines for you – often with just a single mouse click.

Astrology Engine

If you already know your character's date of birth, the program produces a detailed personality profile based on Western and Chinese astrology. You'll discover his strengths, weaknesses, likes, dislikes and much more. If you don't know his date of birth, the program can calculate it based on his main personality traits.

Biorhythm Engine

Biorhythms chart the ups and downs of life and let you see how well (or badly) your characters will perform on a given day. The biorhythm engine examines your character's physical, emotional, intellectual and intuitional status on a daily basis, and explains – in plain English – what it all means. Will the attempted bank robbery succeed, or will it end in miserable failure? If you don't know which way to take the story, the biorhythm engine will help you to decide.

Name Engine

One of the hardest jobs is to come up with names for your characters. The name engine automatically generates male and female names for six different nationalities: UK, USA, French, German, Italian and Spanish.

Story Engine

With a single mouse click, the story engine generates a unique story situation, complete with characters, motivations, locations and objects. You'll never run out of ideas if you use this.

<u>Tarot Engine</u>

The Tarot is a wonderful tool for writers. As with the astrology engine, it doesn't matter whether you believe in it or not. With one click of the mouse, the tarot engine selects ten cards and interprets them for you. Your character's history, problems, hopes, fears, and future are all laid out in front of you. Story ideas will start forming in your mind as soon as you read it.

The next step

You've already learnt plenty of techniques and tricks to get your book finished in double-quick time. But if it still seems like too much hard work, you might be thinking *can't I just cheat?* Well, of course you can. We'll see how in the next two chapters.

14   Cheating (part 1)

Sometimes even a month is too long. You need a book and you need it now. There's no time for research, organising, planning, Mind Maps – or even thinking. Or maybe you're just lazy. Either way, there's only one thing for it – you'll have to cheat.

You'll recognise some of these ideas from earlier chapters, but they're worth repeating here.

Non-fiction in no time

Spend two or three intensive days collecting information. It shouldn't take any longer than that. However unusual the subject, it's unlikely that you're the first person in the world to write about it. Search your library, including the reference section and the children's section. Visit the main county library. Go to an online bookshop such as Amazon and search for books about your subject. Go to a few second-hand bookshops. Buy or borrow a copy of anything that might be relevant.

> Don't worry about the cost of buying books for research. You can sell them on Amazon or eBay when you've finished with them.

Visit local and national newspapers' websites and search their archives. Search for your subject using Google or one of the other search engines. Use Google's groups search facility to search all the newsgroup messages that have been posted over the last few years. Try the *Yellow Pages* or *Thomson's Directory* and see if you can find any companies that might have anything to do with your subject. Call and ask for a brochure, or go along in person and ask questions.

Once you have enough material, all you have to do is copy and paste the best bits into a word processing document. Sort them into logical order, then change the words to match your own writing style and make it all flow nicely – and avoid getting sued for plagiarism.

The easiest way of doing this is to read a paragraph, making sure you understand it, then rewrite it in your own words the way that you would speak it. Don't worry about sounding too formal or informal; you can fix that later. All you're doing now is getting the first draft of the book written as quickly as possible, using your words rather than someone else's.

Another way of doing this is to read a sentence or two from the original text, then rephrase it in your own words and record yourself speaking it onto tape. When you've finished, play back the tape and write down everything you said – or get someone else to do it for you.

When the book is complete – which shouldn't take long – you simply need to edit it as necessary to make it read smoothly and consistently. I recommend printing the book out and marking all the changes with a red pen. Add in any new thoughts that occurred to you along the way. The final step is to update the word processor copy to incorporate the amendments, give it a final read through, then you're done. I recommend getting someone else to read it through as well, just in case you've missed anything – you probably have. See Chapter 18 for more editing ideas.

This might sound like cheating very badly, but it's just a shortcut way of doing what all writers do: lots of research then rewrite the whole thing in your own words, introducing a new angle if possible. All you're doing is speeding up the process. While it might take someone a year to write a book the traditional way, using this method should reduce it to no more than one or two fairly intensive weeks.

Repackaging existing knowledge

Think about your readers. What exactly do they want to know? Make your book a single source of all that information. You can repackage existing knowledge drawn from books, magazines, websites, friends, experts, plus your own ideas, then put it all together in a new form that perfectly suits your target readership. Repackaging is much quicker – and easier – than writing it all from scratch.

As I mentioned above, you will of course need to rewrite other people's work in your own words. You'll also need to do quite a bit of editing – probably more editing than writing – but most people find editing much easier than writing. You should also try to include a few ideas of your own. A book that has something new to say about a subject, or a new angle to offer, is highly saleable. These new ideas are what will make your book unique – but you don't need many of them; one or two per chapter will be plenty.

Write a profile of your target readers to find out what they already know, what they want to know, what sort of level you need to pitch it at, what sort of book they're looking for, and how much they'd be willing to pay. Remember, you were once in their position and knew very little about this subject. What made you become interested? How did you go about learning the basics? How did you extend your knowledge until you reached expert level? Who did you talk to? Who taught you? Are they still around to help you? What made you want to go on learning more?

Carry out a survey of all the other books on the market that cover your subject. What makes your book different, better, easier to understand, more complete, or more up-to-date than any of the others? Try to include more information, more real-life case studies, more interviews with experts, and so on, as well as your own ideas.

Knowing exactly who your readers are means you can repackage a single book into a whole series, each aimed at a different readership: beginners, intermediates, experts, children, teenagers, dog owners, housewives, husbands, single people, executives, and so on. You'll sell many more copies this way, but all you're doing is reusing the same material. It can be rewritten and repackaged very quickly.

How to get other people to write the whole book for you

Think of a great idea for a book and get everyone else to send in contributions for it. All you have to do is sort the contributions into some sort of order, write an introduction and a few paragraphs to link things together, and you're done. In fact, if you can persuade a local dignitary or well-known personality to write the introduction and linking paragraphs, then you might not have to do any writing at all.

Let's say you've come up with a great idea for a book: you'll publish a collection of people's memories and photographs. The book could be about a

If people send you their personal photographs or original documents, be very careful with them and always return them in the same condition as you receive them. Shops that process photographs should be able to copy any you want to keep. Scan or photocopy any other documents and return them immediately.

certain event, a famous or infamous local person, their own town or city, their pets, their first typewriters and word processors, or ... well, I'm sure you get the idea.

So how do you let people know you're looking for contributions? Use your local newspaper (or a relevant specialist magazine). Write in telling them that you're writing a book about whatever subject it is and invite readers to send in their memories, photographs and so on. If it's a quiet week for news – and it often is on local papers – they might even send someone round to photograph you and do an interview.

> When you copy material you intend using in your book, attach a label to the back stating what it is, who sent it to you, and their contact details. Don't write directly on the back as the ink or imprint might show through.

Next comes the hard bit – sorting out everyone's contributions. You might also have to visit your local museum or go through the local newspaper archives to fill in some of the gaps, but that needn't be hard either – especially if you get someone else to do it for you.

Ask a local historian or one of the museum's staff to search the records for you. Go along to the county records office and get one of the assistants to look things up for you. Act 'inept' if necessary, so he takes pity on you. After all, he works there so he should know exactly where to find the information you need. It makes sense to use him rather than doing the work yourself. Tell him you're a writer and you're researching a book; that always gets a good response.

Once the book is finished and ready for publication, get in touch with the newspaper or magazine again. A local writer publishing a book is very big news indeed. You can virtually guarantee that you'll be interviewed and have your photo printed. When you write in to let them know that the book is being published, include a free copy. If the person interviewing you brings the book along, offer to sign it for him. Keep him well supplied with drinks and snacks too. It helps to keep the newspaper on your side – you might get a bigger article and a better review. Remember to tell him where his readers can buy copies of your book.

It doesn't matter whether your book is being published by a mainstream publisher, a small press, or if you're self-publishing it.

Being published is being published as far as local papers are concerned. It's still big news.

Write what you know

How many times have you heard the expression 'write what you know'? You're probably sick of hearing it by now, but it's worth considering if you want to write a book quickly. The more you already know about something, the less research you'll have to do, and the faster and easier it'll be to write about it. Make a list of all the things you know a lot about. Could you write a book about any of those subjects? Perhaps you could incorporate your knowledge into a novel, using it as background detail, or as a clever way to get the hero out of trouble.

Adding padding

Readers of non-fiction books generally like to see plenty of pictures. They help to break up the text, making the books seem more accessible. That's good news if you want to write quickly, because if you can fill up the space with charts, diagrams, photographs, screen-shots, line drawings, cartoons, and so on, then you don't need to write so much.

> One way to get quality illustrations cheaply is to give it to local art students as a project. Tell them exactly what you want, and perhaps make a small contribution to their college or pay for the materials. If they don't get it right first time, make them change it or do it again; it's good practice for when they're in the commercial world. The students benefit too, because they'll have published work to put in their portfolios to show prospective employers.

There are two important things to consider if you take this approach. Firstly, where are you going to get all these images? Unless you can get them for free or produce them yourself, they won't be cheap. And they'll need to be of a professional standard. Secondly, remember that you're always trying to *add value*. And that's exactly what your pictures should do. Use images in place of text by all means, especially where it would take a lot of text to describe something. However, the aim is to make your book at least as informative as it would have been if it was all text. Every picture should therefore be there for a specific reason.

> You should also be able to get free photos and artwork from manufacturers, tourist boards, press offices, publicity agents, and so on. If you're promoting their product or cause in your book, they'll be keen to help in any way they can.

You can also highlight (i.e. duplicate) key points from the text in side panels and boxes. As with pictures, these break up the pages and makes them look more appealing. And they fill up space, so the book seems longer than it really is. You're actually using the same piece of text twice when you do this – a useful trick if your book is a few pages too short.

A better approach, and the one I've adopted in this book, is to make the boxed text different from the main text. As before, the boxes break up the text – and take up space – but now they add value too. You can use this space to give:

- extra tips
- historical facts
- anecdotes
- quotes
- suggestions for further reading
- details of relevant organisations
- explanations
- mini biographies of people mentioned in the text
- and anything else you can think of

And did you see what I just did there? Bullet points! They take up a lot more space than ordinary text, and they create a feeling of space on the page. I used them here because I felt it was the best way of presenting the information.

Guaranteed plots

This one is definitely cheating, but you should get away with it because plenty of other writers have. If you want to write a bestselling novel, where better to find a plot than from another bestselling novel? Don't go for the latest novels; go for something that was a bestseller a few years ago and that most people have forgotten about by. Something between six and nine years old should be about right. You'll find plenty of these in your library, or you can pick them up very cheaply in any second-hand bookshop.

Once you've chosen your bestseller, strip out all the characters, dialogue and description, leaving just the plot. Change the setting, but keep the structure of the story as intact as possible. For example, if you're borrowing the plot of a novel about horse racing at Ascot, you could make yours about greyhound racing in Walthamstow. The subject or theme needs to be similar to the original, but not identical. The location can (and should) be completely different – for speed, choose somewhere you know well. Now add your own characters and dialogue, and replace the description. In a matter of days, the job's done and you've written a great new novel based on a plot that has already proven successful.

Quick, a clone!

Write a clone of a current bestseller. If a recent book has proved successful, then publishers – especially rival companies – will be looking for more of the same as quickly as they can get their hands on it. Use the techniques in this book to write what they're looking for in double-quick time. Don't waste time deliberating over the story and characters – that just gives everyone else a chance to catch up. Change enough details – names, ages, genders, jobs, locations, a few minor plot points – so you can't be sued for plagiarism, then get on with it. If you're concerned about sullying your soon-to-be-famous literary name, use a pen name for this one.

Characters reunited

If you don't have time to invent a completely new set of characters for your latest novel, but you've written other stories in the past, reuse the old characters in your new story. Many writers use the same core set of characters and locations in every book, so why not do the same? To maintain interest, you could introduce a new character from time to time, or kill off an old one, or send one away for a while and bring in a temporary replacement.

> If you need to kill off one of the characters, show it actually happening so the readers get to experience the full horror. Show the other characters reacting, grieving, and sorting out the mess.

Write a series

Many writers end up producing a series of books that feature the same characters and locations every time. It's what readers want and expect – they'd be horrified if their favourite writer wrote something else.

If you don't want to write a series, here's a different approach. The hero or main character in one story doesn't have to be the hero again in the next story. He can still be in the story somewhere, but this time he might be a friend, informant, assistant, lover, or just a minor character in the background. One of the other characters can take over the main role this time.

Another way of avoiding the series problem, but reusing the same characters and locations, is to make each book a self-contained unit, so the story never follows on from one book to the next. Resolve all the issues. Never mention any of the events from one story in another. Since each book stands alone, people can read them in any order.

You also need to consider how much the characters' lives follow on from one book to the next. If a character moves house in one of your stories, what do you do in the next one? Is he back in his old house again, or is he still in his new one? You could perhaps arrange things so that at the end of the house-moving story he has to move back into his old house again. Then there won't be any problem.

But what will you do if you kill off a character? Will you bring him back to life in the next book? Or will he remain dead? I'll let you answer that one.

Recycle your waste

As you've seen, you can reuse characters and locations from other stories. But you could go even further than that. Most writers have plenty of unpublished work hanging around: short stories, articles, poems, novels, and so on. You're just keeping them for sentimental reasons; you can't bear to throw them in the bin.

And if you're a member of a writing group, or if you've ever taken a writing course, then you probably have pages of exercises, character studies, descriptions, short stories, articles, fillers and so on.

Dig them out and read through them all. Remind yourself which scenes you were really proud of at the time, which characters you loved or hated, the settings that are so well described that you can picture yourself there, the articles that have stood the test of time or could be used again with a few tweaks, and so on. You've probably abandoned all hope of ever selling these, but you can rescue the best bits and put them into your book.

Panning for gold, strip mining and weeding

Sometimes you'll read a book and think to yourself what a brilliant story it was. You'd really like to use that idea in a story of your own. That's fine, but the question is what *exactly* is the big idea? What is that one piece of sheer brilliance that you must have in your book?

To find out, you'll need to strip it away layer by layer. Some writers compare this process to weeding a garden. I call in panning for gold – or strip mining. You keep taking out all the things that definitely *aren't* the great idea, until the only thing remaining is the thing you're searching for – that single golden nugget that made the story so wonderful.

Think about the overall theme or genre. Perhaps it was a bit too romantic for your liking. And maybe the jokes didn't really work for you. You'd have liked the story a lot more if it hadn't had all those clowns and circus freaks in it. So strip out the romance, the bad comedy and the circus setting; they obviously aren't what you're looking for. Perhaps the original story was set in Germany, but you think it could have worked just as well anywhere else. So you can discount the location. What about the characters? Go through them one at a time, considering how each one affected you and the impact they had on the story. Discount any that don't really do anything for you, or if a different character would have worked just as well. You're getting closer to the gold now.

Eventually, you're left with the one thing that made you tingle all over. You'll know when you've found it – mainly because it's the only thing left. It might be a concept or a relationship rather than a character or a place or an object. Some examples might be:

- A particular vision of the future which appeals to you.

- Two lovers whose romance is ultimately doomed because of circumstances beyond their control.

- Two people who hate each other fall in love but refuse to admit it.

- The fact that the characters are all animals, ghosts, or inanimate objects.

- The fact that the characters discover their own story recorded in a book and can skip ahead to find out what happens next.

It could be absolutely anything.

Once you've found your golden nugget, it's entirely up to you what you do with it. You could reuse it exactly as it is, change it to make it work in a slightly different way, or turn it around and give it a new twist. Just make sure it still makes you tingle. Then build your new story around it.

ideas4writers.co.uk

This definitely *isn't* cheating, but it does give you a significant advantage over other writers. The ideas database contains thousands of pre-formed ideas for novels and non-fiction books, as well as plots, characters, settings, and entire storylines. Many of the ideas come with examples and variations. Then there are all the What If's. If they don't put your mind into overdrive, then nothing will.

If the ideas in the database aren't quite what you're looking for, you'll also find plenty of suggestions for quick and easy ways to come up with your own. And don't forget the writing engines I mentioned in Chapter 13 – they're so easy to use, it seems like cheating.

The next step

Is it cheating if you get other people to help you write your book? Of course not. In fact, it's quite a traditional thing to do – as we'll see in the next chapter.

15　Cheating (part 2) – using other people

It's good to let other people be involved with your writing. And they like to help. They like to feel that they've contributed to your success. And most importantly, as far as this book is concerned at least, it cuts down the amount of work you have to do to write your book. That means you can write your book much faster – or work on several books simultaneously.

This chapter is all about using other people to help you write your book. Whether you need help with the organising, writing, research, artwork, editing, or someone to talk to when you're stuck, you'll find plenty of people willing to help – if you ask.

So if someone offers to check your facts for you, or do some research while he's in town, or put you in touch with an expert he knows, or maybe even do a spot of proofreading for you, take him up on it – and make sure he actually does it.

A long tradition

In the nineteenth century, when Alexandre Dumas père and his son, Alexandre Dumas fils, wrote their *Boulevard Comedies*, they had twelve writers and two secretaries working for them. This think-tank was an early form of writing team – now commonly used on British soap operas and most American sit-coms.

Dumas père once made a bet that he could write a novel in three days. And he won the bet with six hours to spare. Now, I've had a couple of thoughts about this famous bet. Firstly, Dumas only needed to write the outline and pass it over to his team of writers. Secondly, you don't enter a bet like that unless you already have a good idea of what the story will be about, so he'd probably already written the outline. So all he had to do to win the bet was to hand over the outline to his writers and then go to sleep for three days. Though I'm sure he must have contributed the odd page or two, just to stave off boredom.

Apparently Dumas often left out all punctuation marks too, thus enabling him to write even faster. He relied on his secretaries to insert the punctuation for him.

More recently, Barbara Cartland wrote well over seven hundred books by dictating them to her secretary. You've already seen that dictating is much faster than typing, even if you're a professional typist, and it's considerably faster than writing longhand. And I really can't imagine her poring over manuscripts with a red pen either. Did she really get it spot on first time, or was that another job for her secretary? Or perhaps an editor at the publishing company sorted it all out. However she did it, she saved herself an awful lot of time.

Weekend writing team

Most of us can't afford to retain our own team of writers, of course. You'd have to sell quite a few bestsellers before that could happen. But a secretary, perhaps on a part-time basis, or the use of a secretarial service, is certainly a possibility if a couple of books do well.

In the meantime, you could always share the writing with other writers. These could be members of your local writer's circle, or you could make up a larger group using members from several writing groups in your region. Geography is no boundary in this information age. Let's say there are twenty of you and your book is twenty chapters long. That's one chapter each. If you plan and outline the book properly (see Chapter 7), you should all be able to complete your chapters in one weekend. So between you, you could write fifty-two books a year and have weekdays off (or work your own projects).

It's a lot of fun to work this way, and far more creative than working on your own. And you can get together for regular plotting sessions and progress meetings and bounce ideas around. Again, if geography is a factor, you could hold virtual meetings online.

If your group is planning to write an entire book in one weekend – or even in a week – make sure you let the local media and writing magazines know. They're bound to be interested. And if you succeed, then the news will spread, so plenty of publishers should hear about it too.

Collaborating

Working with another writer on a project might sound like a good idea. Double the writers and halve the work, right? You can bounce ideas off each other, push each other to go faster, and there's always someone to talk to if you're stuck.

Unfortunately, writing with a partner can actually be slower than working on your own. I'm not quite sure why this is, but I've spoken to a number of people who have collaborated with other writers, and they all say the same thing: everything takes longer than you expect.

Naturally, you need to pick your writing partner very carefully. You might be best friends now, but will you still be by the end of the book? Will you even reach the end? What if one of you drops out partway through? How will you resolve your differences?

There are lots of details that you *must* agree on before you begin. And it's best to put everything in writing and both sign it. It saves a lot of trouble later.

Who actually owns the characters? Who owns the setting, the locations, the world? Will either of you be allowed to use these things in other books you write individually? What if you want to kill off one of the characters? Or drop a bomb on one of the cities? What if your partner objects?

Who will do what? How will you divide the earnings? Will you each write alternate chapters? Will one of you write more than the other? How will that affect the earnings? Who will do the editing? What if you want to change something that your partner wants left alone? Whose name will appear on the cover? If both names will appear, whose will appear first? Who will do the interviews and book signings?

In a traditional collaboration, you'll often find yourself waiting for the other person to finish his bit so you can get on with your next bit, and so on. This is where a detailed outline comes in useful once again. Now you don't have to wait for your partner to finish a chapter so you can see how it ended. You already know how it ended, because it's in the outline. That should speed things up.

Professional coaching

Most writers work alone. They even study the art and craft of writing alone. But this isn't the way other professions train their star performers. As soon as someone's talent is recognised – in football or cricket, for example – the able youngster is signed up for a county or national team and given professional coaching. He'll also be expected to put in many long hours of practice.

The same thing applies to writers. You could get there on your own in the end, but unless you're exceptionally lucky, it'll take years. But find yourself a good writing tutor, enrol on a creative writing course, or go to writer's conferences, and you'll get there ten times faster.

Who wants to be a writer?

There's a well-known TV quiz show where you can phone a friend for help if you get stuck. That can work for writers too. Make the effort to cultivate some friendships, and use them to sort out your writing problems. If you were asked a question about the subject of your book, who would you phone if you didn't know the answer?

Sometimes it's good to get away from the writing for a while and clear your head. Discussing the topic you're having problems with in a social context can be a useful way of finding solutions and generating new ideas. You might not even mention that you're a writer. And perhaps you won't mention what you're writing about, or admit you're having problems with it. Just join in the conversation, and gradually, without drawing too much attention to it, steer the subject round to the topic you want to discuss.

If there's a fair or festival where your specialist subject is included, you'll find plenty of like-minded people willing to tell you all they know.

Most people like a good chat. They might not have many hard facts to share, but they'll let you bounce ideas off them, and perhaps chip in with a few thoughts of their own. They might even know someone who has the very information you need – it's surprising how often that happens. So chat to people at weddings and other social occasions, in pubs and cafés, coffee mornings, parent and toddler groups, the canteen at work, or at your next writer's circle meeting. Join a few discussion forums on the internet.

Be my buddy

In many walks of life, getting a friend involved reduces the amount of work, effort, danger, fear, and so on. And it boosts creativity. Two heads are better than one, and the ideas you come up with as a pair can be better than any you could have come up with individually. So, you need someone to bounce your ideas around with – you need a 'buddy'.

Think of schoolchildren holding hands as they cross a road. If you go diving, you should always take a partner – a diving buddy – down with you in case you get into difficulties. Politicians have running mates. Creative teams work together: Lennon and McCartney for example. (Or is it McCartney and Lennon now?)

A ghost!

Most celebrity books are written by ghost writers, and there's nothing to stop you from employing one too – if you can afford their fee. Ghost writers normally spend a few weeks talking to you, collecting background information, going through old letters, notes and photographs and so on, before going away to write the book. You don't need to be able to write or type or even be literate. You'll have full control over what goes in the book and what doesn't, and your name will appear on the cover.

The downside is the expense. Ghost writers will usually demand a flat fee, which could be expensive if the book will take several months to complete. Or they'll take a share of the profits – but only if they know that the book will be a big seller. Or they'll take a demand a flat fee *and* a share of the profits.

If you've led a fascinating life and have a great story to tell about it, then a ghost writer could be a good option. Some publishers will even appoint (and pay for) one for you, especially if they've heard about you through a newspaper or magazine article and want to publish a book about your experiences. Get in touch with as many newspapers and magazines as possible and tell them about the things you've done. Hopefully a book publisher or two will contact you once a few articles have appeared.

You could also let writing magazines know that you have a story worth telling. Perhaps one of their readers might be interested in writing the book for you.

Weirder than you

Here's a fun idea to try if you ever run out of things to talk about with your friends: have a weird ideas contest. The winner is the person who can outdo everyone else and come up with the weirdest, most outrageous, most incredible story or fact. Not real facts of course; these facts will be made up on the spur of the moment.

This is a great game for getting your mind loosened up. And who knows, you might even be able to use some of those weird ideas in your stories, or they might trigger new ideas of your own. Make sure you have your notepad or a tape recorder with you.

Being someone else

How about inventing a new writing persona? It's just like making up a character, but you actually become that character while you write. Your new persona will of course be an extraordinarily talented and prolific writer, able to conjure up wonderful material from any source. He never has any trouble getting started or finding enough time to write. He doesn't get embarrassed about reading his work aloud in front of other people; in fact, he's proud to do so. He loves criticism and treats it as a fantastic learning opportunity. He laughs at rejection letters and sends his work out to the next publisher on his list with a confident, knowing smile. He writes quickly and with great authority. He's led a much richer life than you have, and he's far more knowledgeable. He has an unusually positive outlook and manner, and good fortune seems to seek him out.

Give your new persona a name. It'll be the perfect name for such a talented and successful writer, of course. Become this person every time you go into your writing room. Does he wear a hat, scarf, neckerchief, or smoking jacket? Then you should too. Sit down at your desk and feel yourself changing into him. Your thoughts become more positive, your posture more upright, you feel strong, happy, successful and confident. Now write as he does – quickly, confidently and well.

Six degrees of separation

You may have heard of the principle of six degrees of separation. This principle, which has been proven many times, states that each one of us is just six steps removed from every other person on the planet.

To start the chain, contact the person who you think is the most likely to know the answer (or who might know someone else who would know the answer), and ask them your question. If you can't think of anyone, just ask as many people as possible. What happens next is completely out of your hands. Each person you asked then asks the person they think is most likely to know the answer. And so the chain continues. Your question bounces from person to person, getting ever closer to the person who knows the answer. Within six bounces your question will more than likely have found its way to someone who knows the answer – wherever he is in the world. So if you're woken up in the early hours by a phone call from a very excited professor from the University of Tokyo, who just happens to be the world's foremost authority on that subject, well don't say I didn't warn you.

Friends who listen

Sometimes simply saying a problem out loud is enough to make the answer become apparent. Have you ever asked something and immediately felt foolish as you realised how obvious the answer was? I know I have. The same thing happens when I send emails too. If I'm stuck on a problem, I'll send my friend a message, or post a message on a discussion forum, describing the problem and asking for suggestions. Within seconds of pressing the 'Send' button the answer has come to me. I then have to send another message apologising for being so stupid. Still, it's better to be embarrassed than stuck.

Friends who take care of business

You're a writer, so you should be spending your time writing. You don't want to waste valuable writing time tracking down new publishers and agents or trying to find out the name of an editor. Nor do you want to send out endless query letters. And nor do you want to feel depressed because you've had another rejection.

The solution is to get someone else to look after that side of things for you. He'll do your market research and write query letters for you. He'll compile a list of suitable publisher and agents. He won't get upset when another rejection arrives – it's not his work that's been rejected. He'll simply cross that publisher or agent off his list and send it to the next one. He might not even tell you who he's sent it to or how many rejections you've had. The only time you really need to know is when he's tried every possible publisher and had rejections from all of them, or if he gets an acceptance. It's like having your own personal agent.

Friends who go on holiday

Friends who have been on holiday, or who are about to go, are a valuable resource. Those who've already been will come back with photos, guidebooks, maps and other souvenirs – and plenty of experience and local knowledge. That's just the thing you need to make your exotic settings more authentic. Invite them round, and get them to tell you all about it and show you all their photos and videos. Those who are about to go on holiday are even more valuable because you can give them a shopping list. Tell them what you want them to see, what you want them to photograph or video, particular souvenirs or documents you want them to bring back, and so on. They'll probably be delighted to help.

The pedantic friend

Some people have an opinion on everything. While they usually drive you up the wall, it's at times like this that they can be very useful. Ask them what they know about the subject. Start a lively debate and see if you can come up with a solution between you.

This is also the ideal friend to have when it's time to do the editing. Never show him the first draft, because it's not ready for the public yet. But when you've finished polishing it, hand it over to him and see what he makes of it. Pedantic friends are generally very good at English, so if he finds any mistakes he'll mark them very clearly. That's exactly what you want; it's better that somebody spots these errors now, before the rest of the world gets to see them.

As you write more books, you'll find yourself trying harder to fix all the mistakes before your pedantic friend sees them. When he can't find anything wrong, you'll know you've finally cracked it. But he'll *always* find something wrong. Guaranteed.

Is there an artist in the house?

Artwork can be horrendously expensive. If you're a novelist, you might not need any artwork – unless you're planning to self-publish your book and need an attractive cover. Non-fiction writers, on the other hand, often need charts, illustrations, cartoons, screenshots, photographs, maps, and so on. And again, if you're planning to self-publish, you might also need a nice picture for the cover.

You could go to a commercial artist, graphic designer or photographer for your artwork – if you're rich. Or you could leave it up to the publisher, though they probably won't be too happy about this, and it could reduce your chances of getting published.

So the obvious solution is to use other people. I mentioned in the previous chapter that you could get local art students to do some work for you as a project. You could also ask your friends, family, work colleagues and other acquaintances if they know someone with a talent for art or photography. They probably do; there are as many budding artists in the world as there are writers.

You can create a lot of art on computers these days, especially if you have a digital camera. You don't need to be a trained artist to get fantastic results; you just need the right equipment and to know how to use it. Some idea of what you're trying to achieve also helps. If you don't have the equipment, the ability, or the time to learn, there are plenty of people who do. Ask around and you'll probably receive several enthusiastic offers of help. Art is fun – and the chance of seeing your work published in a book makes it even more so.

More jobs for friends

What else could a friend do for you? Well, as I've mentioned previously, if you've dictated your book, handwritten it, or written it in shorthand, then he could type it up for you. If he has good English skills, he could proofread your book for you. If his English skills are *really* good then he could even edit it for you.

If your partner moans that you spend too much time writing and you never do things together any more, that's another great opportunity. Send her on an editing or proofreading course!

Thanking friends

A loyal team of helpers can save you hundreds of hours of researching, writing, editing and paperwork. They might even allow you to achieve things that would have been impossible on your own. Make sure you thank them properly. Then they'll be happy to do it all over again.

Here are just a few of the many ways in which you could thank them:

- A signed copy of your book.

- A mention in the acknowledgements section.

- Hold a party when the book is finished.

- Invite them to the launch party.

- Name your characters after them – with permission of course.

- Buy them lunch – but pick their brains for ideas while you're there.

- Buy them a small gift.

- Buy them a more expensive gift if they can use it to help you (an encyclopaedia, a digital camera).

- Pay for them to attend a writing, editing or proofreading course – which will make them even more useful to you.

- Just say thanks.

The next step

It's unlikely that you'll suffer from writer's block if you use the techniques in this book. But just in case you do, the next chapter is stuffed with tips on how to avoid it and how to overcome it.

16   Writer's block

So, you've come to a complete standstill. You can't write another word. You haven't got a clue what you're going to write next. Your mind is blank. You'll never be able to write again. Your talent has deserted you – possibly forever. Perhaps you never had any talent in the first place. Welcome to the wonderful world of writer's block.

Back to the outline
If you're following an outline, you should always know exactly where you are and what comes next. So if you've got writer's block, the most likely problem is that you haven't broken the outline down into enough detail. In Chapter 7, I recommended breaking down the outline to the point where you could write each step with five minutes of thinking time followed by ten or fifteen minutes of writing time. It's worth reading that chapter again, because those techniques are the foundation of everything else in this book.

The other possibility is that there's something seriously wrong with your outline and your subconscious is telling you to stop and sort it out. Review your outline, and make sure you've covered everything and it all flows logically.

And remember another tip from earlier in the book: don't write a word until you've thought it through in your head. If the words aren't there yet, there's no point trying to write anything; you obviously need more thinking time. If it's a really tricky section, you might need to spend several five-minute thinking sessions on it until you get it right. They won't all be as bad as that.

Deadlines
Deadlines are a great way of breaking writer's block. You have to get a certain piece of work finished by that time – or else. It has to be a serious deadline though. If you seriously believe you could miss the deadline by an hour, a day, a week, or even a couple of months, and it won't make any difference, then it won't work. But if you'll definitely

lose the publishing deal if your work isn't there on time, or if your contract will be cancelled, or if you'll be sacked, then that's a serious deadline. You'll work your socks off to meet it, even if it means staying up all night. That's the sort of deadline you need.

What if you don't have a deadline? Here's an idea: tell as many people as possible the date when your book will be finished. If you don't make it in time, you'll be a laughing stock. Or you could do what Alexander Dumas did and bet hard cash on your ability to finish it in time. The bigger the bet, the faster you'll write!

You are a supercomputer

Imagine a computer programmed to calculate something very complex – such as the plot, characters, dialogue, viewpoints, locations, motivations, goals, interactions, emotions, theme, structure, clues, red herrings, flashbacks, traps, escapes, thrills, jokes, cliff hangers and climax that make up a novel. You'd expect it to take some time. Your brain is more powerful than a supercomputer, but there are still limits as to what's possible. There are a lot of calculations to be done, and the amount of time required could be considerable.

You might interpret this period of *necessary thinking time* as being blocked, but you aren't blocked really. Your brain will let you know when it's finished the calculations. You'll suddenly have an urge to write again. And you'll soon make up the time you lost because you thought you were blocked.

Ditch the word processor

Try writing in Microsoft Outlook or Outlook Express rather than your word processor. See Chapter 10 for details.

How good a writer are you really?

Do you ever doubt your writing ability? Then you need a second opinion – and preferably a professional one. See Chapter 10.

There are three possible outcomes: your writing is bad, or it needs improvement, or it's good.

If it's bad, you could take a writing course – or admit that writing isn't really your thing. You could still be a storyteller or a teacher or speechmaker, especially if you have an urge to communicate. And you could record yourself on tape and then have it typed up, so you could still write books.

If your writing needs improvement, you'll need to find out which parts are the weakest. Once you know that, you can take writing courses and read books that focus on those particular aspects. Do lots of writing exercises to practise those skills until you can do them well.

If someone who's qualified to pass judgement tells you your writing is good, then you know you're doing it right. That should give you a tremendous confidence boost – and hopefully be enough to lift your writer's block.

Editing comes later

As I've said throughout the book, writing and editing are completely separate processes that use different parts of the brain. You should never try to do both at the same time; that's just asking for trouble. For now, focus on getting the book written and ignore the errors.

Hop, skip and jump

One of the many advantages of a detailed outline is that you can skip about as you write the book; you don't have to write it in sequential order. If you're having problems with a particular section, skip it for now and do the parts you can write easily.

When you've completed all the easy parts, you'll need to go back and fill in the gaps. Think about why you left each gap. Did you think that section would be difficult to write? Did you try writing it and give up? Could you write it now? If so, go ahead.

But what if this section still looks difficult? Think about why it seems so hard. Do you really need to write it? Could you summarise it, or gloss over the details, or simply leave it out? Can you think of something better to put there instead? Is this section in the right place? Should it come earlier or later in the book? Or does it belong in a different book?

Always writing

Most writers find that when they're writing, thoughts flow quite easily. It's when they stop writing that they have trouble. The secret, then, is to not stop writing. Keep two word processing documents open. When you get stuck, switch to the other document and write about the section you're stuck on, why you think you're stuck on it, various directions you could take, how you got to that point, and so on. If nothing comes to mind, just write your name over and over again. Don't stop writing even for a second.

When the ideas start flowing again, switch back to your main document and carry on writing. If the ideas still aren't flowing after several minutes, stop writing and look at what you've just written. You might have found several ways forward without realising it. Or perhaps you've identified a specific problem that needs to be resolved before you can carry on.

There's no business like... writing

Treating writing like a business should help you to overcome most problems with writer's block. Imagine a journalist writing up a story he has no interest in. He'll have to write it anyway if he wants to keep his job. See Chapter 10 for more about this.

Positive mental attitude

Writer's block is often simply a matter of losing confidence in your writing ability, losing confidence in yourself, or letting the thought of success scare you. It happens to all of us from time to time. Even successful writers sometimes believe they became successful by mistake and they'll eventually be found out. And many highly successful actors suffer from stage fright, or develop it later in their careers.

Fortunately, there are plenty of ways to recover your confidence. Let's look at some of them:

Self-help books

A book on improving your self-confidence will probably include several exercises for you to try. Don't skip them. You won't recover your self-confidence just by reading the book. You need to practise the exercises in a safe environment, building up your confidence until you no longer have a problem.

Of course, you don't just want to recover your old self-confidence; you want to have more. Look out for books that show you how to gain *supreme self-confidence*. It'll take time and effort to achieve this, but by then you'll be able to handle anything – including TV and radio appearances, lectures, book signings and all the other things you might need to do to promote your book.

Self-hypnosis

Hypnosis sessions can be expensive, and you need to repeat them regularly to get the maximum effect. Fortunately, self-hypnosis is just as effective and is considerably cheaper and more convenient. You usually get a tape or CD, and all you have to do is relax and listen. Some people go into a trance, some don't. Some fall asleep, some don't. It doesn't matter what happens; it should work anyway.

I can particularly recommend two of Paul McKenna's products: *Positivity* and *Supreme Self Confidence*. Positivity is a ten-CD boxed set that includes Supreme Self Confidence, so you don't need both. The Positivity boxed set also includes *The Power of a Positive Perspective*, which I find very effective. As far as I know, that one isn't available separately.

When I first tried the Positivity system, I was feeling tired, a little depressed, and extremely annoyed about something that had happened earlier in the day. I didn't really think that listening to a CD would make the slightest difference. But when the CD ended, I felt wide-awake, full of energy and ready to take on anything. I didn't feel as if I'd been in a trance. But whatever had been causing those negative thoughts now seemed so insignificant that it wasn't worth thinking about anymore, and I soon forgot all about it.

It's taken me up to three weeks to get over things like that before, so that was a pretty impressive outcome for one session. The instructions say you're supposed to listen at least five times during the first week, which I did. I've also found I need to listen to it again once every few weeks, otherwise the negative thoughts start to return. I certainly notice the difference if I skip it for a couple of months – and so does my wife!

Unfortunately, both Positivity and Supreme Self Confidence are quite hard to find these days. However, at the time of writing, Supreme Self Confidence is available from Amazon.co.uk as a used product, and Positivity is available on eBay.co.uk.

Supportive friends

A good way of regaining confidence in your writing ability is to get your friends and family to help you. Give them some examples of your writing – either from your current book or from previous writing projects – and tell them you're only looking for *positive* comments. Ask them which bits they liked best and why, which bits are particularly well written, and so on. There's a time and a place for criticism, but this isn't it, so if they find any errors or badly written sections, ask them not to tell you about them on this occasion.

Now go through all the comments you received and write the best ones on a single page that you can refer to when things get tough.

Pin ups

Try enlarging some examples of your best work and stick them on the walls around your room, together with the positive comments you received about them.

Success is it's own reward

There's nothing like a bit of success to give your confidence a boost. Success at writing proves you have talent and you're doing it right.

There are three main ways of proving your writing ability:

- Getting published.

- Winning a competition, or being chosen as a runner-up.

- Receiving praise from qualified people – writing tutors, agents, editors, or professional writers, for example.

Until you have that proof, you'll always have a nagging doubt about your writing ability. You need to get rid of that doubt as soon as possible, as it will inhibit your writing and could lead to writer's block. What you need are a few 'quick wins' – and the best way of getting them is to write short stories and magazine articles.

It's worth spending some time – six to twelve months perhaps – writing as many short stories and articles as you possibly can. Research the magazine markets: find out who their readers are, the types of stories and articles each magazine prefers, and so on. Then target your work accordingly. This subject alone would fill an entire book – and there are plenty of books available, so please read some. You should also enter as many short story competitions as you can.

Remember, you're not doing this to make money; you just want confirmation of your writing ability. A single sale or competition win will be enough. However, you'll be competing against hundreds of other writers, so it's very unlikely that you'll succeed straight away.

If you've had no success after a year, consider taking a writing course. See the Resources section for details of some of the better ones.

Change your wallpaper

Some people say they've collected enough rejection slips to cover their walls. Now that wouldn't be a very positive thing to do. Who wants to be reminded of their failures? Start covering your walls with acceptances instead. It'll take you much longer to collect these of course, but it's worth the wait. You might have a few already, from earlier books, short stories, poems or magazine articles that have been published. Stick them up on your wall so you can see them every day. Doesn't that make you feel better?

And don't just hang up the acceptance letters – hang up a copy each piece of work that was accepted too. You're building a gallery of success – proof that you really can do it.

And relax

If you're suffering from writer's block, you're also suffering from stress and tension. That might be the cause of your writer's block, or it might be the result of it. Either way, you want to get rid of it.

A relaxing bath can work wonders. But how about going a stage further and lighting the room with scented candles? And while you're at it, put some herbal bath oils in the water, and listen to something soothing.

You might remember the natural sound recordings I mentioned earlier. I've got a bubbling stream one, which is great for drowning out noise, and one of a boat drifting in a calm bay with waves lapping gently at the sides – very relaxing when you're in the bath. If you want something more inspiring, try listening to a recording of thunderstorms, or waves crashing against rocks.

Healthy competition

Have you tried talking to your partner about your writer's block? Or you could try talking about some other problem you're having – a hero who's stuck down a hole, or the best way of explaining something very technical. Anything's worth a try when you're stuck. Occasionally they'll come up with the perfect solution, but most of the time they won't understand the situation as well as you do, so their suggestions will seem worthless. But that's OK. Their poor ideas should trigger your natural competitiveness. You'll try to go one better, and your own ideas will start to form.

I'm scared of succeeding

You might have writer's block because you're scared of success. It can happen. What will my friends and family think? What would my mother think? Or my gran? What if they want me to go on TV or do a book signing tour? I couldn't do that; I'd be so embarrassed.

Fortunately, there are several solutions:

- Don't tell anyone you're writing anything.

- Use a pen name.

- Tell your publisher you don't want to take part in any publicity – and that means no author's photo on the back cover, no book signings, and no interviews.

- Get someone else to act on your behalf and do all the publicity, while you remain invisible behind the scenes.

Perhaps you'll come out of hiding and use your real name when you're sure your writing will be well received. If you used a pen name, you could use both your real name and your pen name on the next book: Stan Bean writing as Martina Moog, for example.

Another option, if you're scared of success, is to do something slightly dangerous. How about a sponsored parachute jump, or abseiling down a tall building? Being a successful writer will seem quite tame in comparison.

Take a break

You can take a complete break from writing but still remain creative. In the case of fiction, you could draw or doodle pictures of your characters, paint a cover design for your book, paint a scene from the story, draw maps of all the locations, write a poem about your story, choose quotes to go at the start of each chapter, and so on. In the case of non-fiction, you can also paint a cover design, but you might also need other illustrations and photographs for your book, so now would be a good time to sort that out.

You'll return to your writing feeling refreshed and inspired, with plenty of new ideas and a clearer understanding of where things are going.

A final tip

Remember, if you're severely blocked, don't go anywhere near your word processor, typewriter or notepad. You need to plan the exact words you're going to write in your head before you write them down. If all you can manage is a single sentence, that's fine. Don't worry about it. Just write it down, switch the machine off, and start thinking about the next sentence. Maybe you'll write that one tomorrow. It's a painfully slow way of writing, but at least you *are* writing. It's better to be writing slowly than to be worrying about not writing at all. Gradually your urge to write will kick back in. Perhaps, when you're writing tomorrow's sentence, you'll think of a great second sentence and you'll write it there and then. Terrific – you're fighting back. You'll soon be back up to full speed.

The next step

That's your writer's block sorted out, but you might still be having trouble staying motivated. We'll deal with that in the next chapter.

17   Staying motivated

Rewards and motivators

Be proud of what you achieve in each writing session. Give yourself a reward if you feel you've accomplished something worthwhile. Play a tape of a crowd applauding, or perhaps a rousing burst of the Hallelujah Chorus. Have a chocolate biscuit as you bask in the glory of a job well done. Or keep a joke book nearby, and celebrate with laughter.

Focus on success

What do you hope to achieve by writing books? To give up your job? To be wealthy and live in a castle? To travel the world meeting interesting people – and get paid for it? Is it the fame? Or do you want to be remembered by future generations? Everyone is different. Decide what your own reason is, then focus on achieving it.

Find pictures that represent your success, and surround yourself with them. If you want to travel, hang maps and photos of the places you want to visit on your wall where you can see them every day. If you want to live in a castle, find one you like and hang a picture of it on your wall. If you want to be wealthy, use your computer to make a fake bank statement that shows you're worth millions. Look at it regularly, so you get used to seeing it. If you want to give up work, decide what you want to do instead and start doing some of those things now, as if you'd already left. Focusing over and over again on the things you really want will have a positive effect on you. Things will start to happen; success will find you.

Past successes

List all your past successes: books, articles, stories, plays and poems you've written, work that's been published, competitions you've won or been a runner-up in, and so on. Include successes from other areas of your life too: children you've raised, jobs you've done well, successful interviews, exams, promotions, things you've achieved, things you've been complimented on, and so on. You should be starting to feel pretty good about yourself. You've achieved so much – and you can do it again.

The evil ones
Make a list of the people who are more successful than you. And note their ages. Yes, some people who are more successful than you are also much younger than you. And some are much older. Doesn't that make you want to get writing again? Show the world you're just as good as they are – if not better.

Hitting the target
Remember that you always need a target to aim for. See Chapter 10 for details.

Finished already
Imagine that you've already completed your book. It's a big success. You're on stage accepting an award for it. Everyone's applauding. People are on their feet cheering. Think about how good that feels. As you set yourself goals and deadlines, imagine that you've already achieved those too.

If you keep imagining yourself being successful, your brain will eventually come to believe you *are* successful. Success is like money – it always goes to those who already have it. Once you start truly believing that you're successful, real success will soon follow. Many people have tried this technique and found it really does work. It's got to be worth a try.

Repeat after me...
Try repeating the same phrase *out loud* ten times. Do it several times a day. Saying it out loud means that you hear it as well as think it. That reinforces the message and encourages success. Choose a very specific phrase to repeat. If you're having problems writing the book, try: "I, [name], will finish writing [title of book] by [specific date]". If you're having doubts about how successful it will be, try: "My book, [title of book], will win [name of award] by [specific date]." Or "My book, [name of book], will sell [large number] copies by [specific date]."

As you repeat your phrase, picture yourself achieving the thing you're talking about. How good does it feel? Very good indeed, I hope.

Visualise every detail of it. Wallow in success. As we've seen above, you need to convince yourself that what you're saying is true. When you truly believe it, it will become true. This process is called affirmation and is well worth studying further if you're interested in it. It certainly works for me. And it can also be used for other things, such as healing.

I recently came up with a more advanced version of affirmation, and its power astonished me. It left me feeling quite exhilarated. I don't know if this version has been discovered by anyone else – if not, then I claim full credit.

In this version, you don't speak the words out loud, but close your eyes and imagine them being spoken by other people. Start with yourself, then add the other people in your house, then everyone in your street, all saying the words at the same time, like a chant. And not just saying the words, but *believing* them too. Keep expanding outwards: everyone in your town, in your county, in your region, in the whole country, and then everyone in the world. Now the whole world is willing you to succeed; you can hear them all chanting it simultaneously in every country. It's loud, but not deafening. And everyone is smiling and happy. Keep repeating the phrase, but this time zoom in on specific people – celebrities, people you admire, family and friends, people you know and trust. See them looking directly at you, and hear their actual voices speaking your phrase, reassuring you that it will definitely happen.

How do you feel at the end of that session? Pretty good, I bet. You're left in no doubt that the words you're saying will definitely come true. The first time I tried it, the thing I wanted to happen did indeed happen – in under four hours!

A poem a day

For an inspiring way of starting the day, try reading a short poem as soon as you wake up each morning. A good poem will inspire you and brighten your day. You'll also absorb the imagery and rhythms, which will filter into your writing style and make it seem more lyrical and alive.

You might also like to read a poem each night just before you go to sleep. You could pick the same one you read that morning, or perhaps the one you'll read tomorrow morning. Or choose something else – something very imaginative to inspire some interesting dreams.

More motivation tips

- Try sticking some inspirational words, phrases and quotes around the room. Make them nice and big so you can see them from your writing desk.

- You could also stick up photos of people whose success or lifestyle you admire.

- Go to a motivation workshop. These are more common in the USA than in the UK, but they're gradually becoming more popular, especially with business people and sales teams. Writers can benefit too.

Longer writing sessions

Sometimes, if you're in a creative mood and you have plenty of time to spare, it's nice to indulge yourself with a really long writing session. It can take up to thirty minutes to settle into a long session though, so start with a couple of mini-sessions so you're immediately productive.

After that, try writing the next section without pre-planning it in your head. This is the more traditional way of writing, but when you're really 'in the groove' the words will flow easily.

If you're writing fiction, the characters can take on a life of their own – all you have to do is write down what they do or say. These sections are usually 'right first time' and will need little or no editing.

Many writers find that their characters sometimes take over and the story goes off in a completely different direction. If that's what you want to happen then that's fine, but it's not the best way if you want to write your book quickly. If it drifts too far from the storyline and then fizzles out, you'll have to scrap that entire section and write it again.

Keep the current section of the outline firmly in your mind as you write. Then you should find that the characters stick to the storyline.

The next step

At last the first draft is finished. There's still plenty of work to do to bring it up to a professional – and publishable – standard though. So in the next chapter we'll edit your book – in the fastest possible time of course.

18 Editing

In this chapter, we'll look at some ideas, tips and techniques for making the editing process as fast and effective as possible. It should take you less than two weeks to turn your first draft into a professionally written book that's ready for publication.

There's a time and a place

Writing is a creative process, and if you're at your most creative in the morning then you're unlikely to be at your most logical and analytical then; that's probably the afternoon or evening for you. So that's when you should be doing the editing. If, like me, you're more creative in the evening, you'll probably make a better job of editing in the daytime.

If you don't have the luxury of being able to work at different times of the day, you should at least keep writing and editing separate and not try to combine them in a single session.

Another important point to consider, if you're working at a different time of day, is the place. If you're at your most analytical in the daytime but the house is very noisy then, you might decide to do the editing somewhere else – the reference room in the library, for example.

Work, rest and edit

In the writing section of this book, I advocated using mini-sessions. For editing though, I recommend a two-hour session. Unfortunately, these are more difficult to fit into a normal day. You can get around this by setting aside a week or two to edit your book. That might mean taking a week off work, videoing all TV programmes, using a child-minder, and so on.

Don't edit for more than two hours at a time. When you're feeling awake and alert, you're far more critical and only the best writing passes muster. But the longer the session, the more tired you get. You become lazy and permissive; mistakes and sloppy writing slip through. If you notice your standards slipping, then it's definitely time for a break.

Editing isn't for me

Editing isn't for everyone. And you might be itching to get on with your next book. Many professional writers feel the same way. Some have secretaries to do their editing for them. Others use their partner or rely on an agent or editor.

Unless you already have an agent or editor, your best bet is to contact an editorial agency such as:

- Jacqui Bennett Writer's Bureau
- The Hilary Johnson Authors' Advisory Service
- The Literary Consultancy

You'll find contact details for these agencies in the Resources section.

If you're planning to self-publish your book, sending it away for a professional polish is a must. You don't want to spend hundreds or even thousands of pounds publishing something that's full of mistakes.

In fact, many writers send their work to one of these agencies as a matter of course, even if they're planning to approach a mainstream publisher. A professional editorial agency will give your book an extra polish that will significantly increase your chances of getting it published.

Wait for a month

The errors in your book won't stand out at this stage, because you're too close to the work. If you tried to edit the book now, you'd miss many of them. So put your first draft away and get on with writing your next book. When the first draft of that one is completed, come back and edit this one. Or you could just have a month off.

Edit-ability

It's worth brushing up your English skills just before you begin the editing process. Read a book on grammar and punctuation to remind yourself of the finer points, such as the correct use of commas, semi-colons, and colons; when to use 'compared to' and when to use 'compared with'; punctuation within speech marks; and so on.

When I were a lad...

As time passes, English usage changes. So make sure any guides you refer to are recent editions, not something you've had on your shelf since the 1970s. For example, most people use fewer commas these days – although I still prefer the old way. And single quotes are generally preferred to the double quotes most of us learnt at school. A few hours spent reading a modern guide to English style and usage could prove quite a revelation.

The masterclass in your hand

If you find yourself getting stuck when editing your work, pick up a recently published novel or non-fiction book that you consider to be well written, and compare it to yours. If you choose a book from one of the publishers you're planning to send your book to, that's even better. This is a quick way of checking elements of style, such as quotes and speech marks (single or double), spellings (ise/ize), punctuating dialogue, and so on.

Some shared advice

Most professional writers develop their own method of editing. Some even share their method with the rest of the world. Of particular note, not just for editing, but for writing advice in general, is Holly Lisle's website (www.hollylisle.com).

When a book dies

Sadly, some books never make it. Days of fiddling turn into weeks of rewrites, and it's still not working. Eventually, you finally realise that this book was never meant to be. It happens to all of us. Forget about it and write another one.

I once had three books in a row die on me. Two years wasted. I didn't know how to write books quickly in those days either. I gave up writing for a few years and developed an interest in computers instead. As it turned out, that was actually a good thing. Eventually, I returned to writing because I'd had a fantastic story simmering in my brain for months. And that one didn't die.

Complete the first draft

The first stage of the editing process is simply to go through your notes and add in any extra bits, or make any changes you noted during the writing stage. You'll also need to expand any abbreviations into full text, complete any partial sentences, and so on.

A complete read-through

Before you make any more changes, read through the whole book from start to finish. This will give you a good idea of how well everything fits together. Has the book achieved all of its objectives? Did every loose thread get resolved? Does it have a definite beginning, middle and end? Is the ending satisfying and logical? Is every scene, character and line of dialogue there for a reason?

Spell check on

Throughout the writing process, you should have had your spell checker turned off so you weren't tempted to make corrections. Now you can turn it back on and go through each chapter fixing all the spelling mistakes. To turn on the spell checker in Microsoft Word, click on the Tools menu, choose Options, go to the Spelling and Grammar page and tick the box labelled 'Check spelling as you type'. If the box labelled 'Hide spelling mistakes in this document' is ticked, click on it to remove the tick, then click the OK button.

An alternative method is to press the F7 key or click the spell check button on the toolbar. This brings up a separate window that takes you through every error in the document.

Unfortunately, spell checkers won't catch errors such as using *there* instead of *their*. That needs a human eye – and the more eyes (i.e. people) you have checking for errors, the better.

Edit on paper, not on screen

The next stage is to print the whole book out. Don't try to edit it on your computer; you'll miss too many mistakes. You really do need a printed copy of your book to work from.

You'll be scrawling all over the text, making corrections, leaving notes, rewriting sentences and so on, so leave plenty of room. Print on one side of the paper only, use wide margins, and set the line spacing to double-spaced.

I always use a red pen for editing, but as long as you can clearly see the changes you've made it doesn't matter what colour you use. You'll need a good quality pen that writes smoothly and doesn't blob or stop dead. A poor quality pen will slow you down and

> You might be able to get away with 1.5 line spacing if you need to save paper – try printing a single page in that format and see if you can edit it comfortably.

cause endless aggravation, so it's worth shopping around and finding a decent one.

Later, once you've completed the editing, take the amended printout to your word processor and make all the changes on screen. When you've finished making these changes, print the whole thing out and read it through again. This time you'll be looking for the odd little glitches. Hopefully there won't be too many of these – but there are bound to be some, so it's worth doing. This time you can save paper by using single spacing and narrow margins. You could even print on both sides of the paper if your printer can do that.

Consistency

Characters are allowed to change during the course of your story, but these changes must be accounted for in the text. If your heroine starts off as a shrew-like brunette but ends up as an assertive blonde, you must show her personality developing – and you might need a scene set in a hair salon too!

Before you start writing, prepare a continuity card for each character that lists their main features: hair and eye colour, age, height, accent, motivation, temperament, behaviour, mannerisms and habits, and so on. Refer to these cards as you write and you should never make any mistakes. If you mention a new feature, add it to that character's card immediately. It makes checking for consistency so much easier.

So the next step in the editing process is to read through the book again, cross-checking every character's details against their card.

Major revision

Major revision is where whole scenes, or even entire chapters, need to be added, deleted or moved around. If your book was well planned and organised before you started writing it, and you stuck rigidly to the outline, then you won't need to make any major changes, so I'm not going to spend too much time on this topic.

As you read through the text, you might have some great ideas for new characters, extra subplots, new obstacles and complications, and all sorts of other things. Don't even think about putting them into this book. Write them down and save them for the next one. The current story is finished. All you're doing now is polishing it, not changing it. You could go on making changes forever and never be completely satisfied. Some people actually do that, and never finish writing their book. Don't be one of them. Polish this book, make it the best it can possibly be, then move on to the next one.

Minor revision

This is where you'll focus most of your efforts during the editing process. There are lots of little details you need to check, including:

- Clichés: avoid them like the plague, except in dialogue.

- Clues and red herrings: did you plant these in the right places? Did you remember to follow them up later in the story?

- Conflict: there should be some on every page.

- Confused words: their/there/they're, idle/idol, weak/week, your/you're, and so on. Your spell checker won't spot these. Your readers will.

- Descriptions: change generic words and phrases to specific ones. Avoid words such as 'very', 'nice', 'tree', 'flower'.

- Facts: double-check every single one. Don't rely on a fact you found on someone's website – they might have got it wrong. Go to the original source of the information if possible.

- Foreshadowing: go back a few scenes and plant clues about what's coming. Build tension

- Location: does the character actually go to the place he was supposed to?

- Numbering conventions: have you started off using words (Chapter One) but then switched to numbers (Chapter 12)?

- Overused words: and, that, I, said, he, she, just, the, but, then, so. Some are necessary, but probably not all of them.

- Scenes: have a beginning, middle and end; are set in *one* place at *one* time; contain conflict; use a single viewpoint.

- Senses: enhance your descriptions by using more of your senses: sight, smell, touch, taste, sound. Use vivid words that match the mood.

- Speech marks: have you used double quotes or single quotes consistently? Use one or the other, but not both.

- Spelling, grammar, and punctuation.

- Timeline: has the right amount of time elapsed between a character leaving one place and arriving somewhere else?

- Unnecessary words: totally, utterly, completely, and so on. To say that someone is *completely dead* is the same as saying they're *dead*. Half dead is OK though – it's how I feel after two hours in the gym!

A little remodelling

- Try rephrasing every sentence to see if you can make it better. Your word processor's grammar checker might suggest a 'correct' version, but don't just assume it's right.

- Words at the beginning and end of each sentence are in the strongest positions, so move the most important words there. Similarly, sentences at the beginning and end of each paragraph are in the strongest positions and are therefore the most likely to be remembered.

- Delete unnecessary words.

- Check the revised sentence's meaning and context. Does it still say what you intended? Does it still fit in with the surrounding sentences?

Active scenery

You can enhance your description of a setting by adding movement. Think of your story as a movie: waves wash against the shore, trees and bushes blow in the wind, vehicles go by, people go about their business, and so on. Turn your backgrounds into mini movies and bring them to life.

Advanced find and replace

If you have Microsoft Word, use the advanced find and replace functions to highlight particular words – see the list of overused words above. Pick a word such as 'that' and replace it with the same word but with the font set to red, bold and highlighted. Every occurrence of that word now stands out a mile, making it easy to assess each one and decide whether to keep it or delete it. If you tend to overuse commas or exclamation marks, do the same for them.

Another pair of eyes

As I said above, you've become so close to your book now that you only read what you *think* is there, not what's *actually* there. So don't ever send your work off to a publisher without letting at least one other person read it. Choose someone with excellent English skills – an English teacher would be a good choice. And it's even better if he's really pedantic. You'll be surprised how many mistakes you missed.

Be a perfectionist

If something isn't quite right, or is niggling you, fix it now or you'll always regret it. Don't be satisfied until your book is as perfect as you can make it. Could someone else have done a better job? If so, think about what would they have done differently, then try your hardest to bring your book up to their standard. Perfection takes time, but it brings its own rewards: the satisfaction of a job well done, a glow of pride, and a much better chance of getting published.

Be brutal

If you take things gently, you'll only have to go through it all again later – and that's something we're trying to avoid if we're editing quickly. You'll save time by doing it properly in the first place. That means being brutal and cutting ruthlessly.

Cutting it down to size

Editing generally means cutting. Nobody likes to throw away good writing, but if it doesn't fit the current book then it has to go. You might even have to cut parts you love. Your finished book should be tightly written, with every character, scene, line of dialogue and description there because it *has* to be.

But how much should you cut? Find a writing competition that specifies a word count. Write the story, then see how much over (or under) the word count you are. Having done this myself, I know that I overwrite by about forty-five percent, so that's how much I need to cut from each piece of writing.

It's a good idea to set up a 'good bits' folder for all the things it really hurts you to cut. If you had nowhere else to store these pieces, you'd be tempted to leave them in, even though they don't really belong. But with a 'good bits' folder, you can cut them out and save them for other projects. That means you can be as ruthless as you like and not worry that you've wasted something special.

Instinct

For maximum speed, always go with your first instinct. That way, it should sound natural, just as if you were speaking it.

More detail means more importance

Examine every sentence, every word, every phrase, and every description and consider whether it's actually relevant. Have you described an object in the background that has no real significance in the story? Why? The more detail you add, the bigger the role the reader expects that thing to play.

Put paid to the passive

In fiction, your main characters should be the ones carrying out the actions, so they should always appear first in the sentence. For example, don't say: A woman was having her hair cut by Maureen.

Write: Maureen was cutting a woman's hair. Or you could liven things up considerably by using a more interesting verb: Maureen *hacked* at the woman's hair… and a clump the size of a small cat came away in her hand.

Say it out loud

Does your writing sound as good as it looks? Does the rhythm sound right, or does it seem jerky? Do you get out of breath because the sentences are too long? You can improve the quality of your writing quite significantly by reading the words aloud. But if you really want to polish it to perfection, you need to hear it read by someone else. Now the errors really stand out. You might even find yourself cringing at the awkward phrasing, clichés, vague descriptions, and continuity errors.

If that sounds too embarrassing, use a text-to-speech computer program. Dragon NaturallySpeaking, which we looked at earlier, includes RealSpeak which reads your text back to you. Or you can get standalone programs such as Natural Voice Reader.

The long and winding description

Instead of using several weak words to describe something, try to find a single strong word. For example: ran slowly = jogged; ran quickly = sprinted. This helps your readers to create a much clearer picture in their minds. They should see the scene exactly as you do. Also, try using *pictorial* words that instantly conjure up a certain image in your reader's mind.

Once your readers have a clear picture of a character in their minds, don't keep reminding them what he looks like. You only need an occasional word or two when it's important that they remember a specific detail.

Time and place

If you've ever seen a film script, you'll know that each scene starts with a line that identifies the location and time of day. It's useful to mark up the scenes in your novel in this way too. This makes it easy to check that your story's timeline flows correctly, and all your characters are where you expected them to be. Erase these lines when you've finished editing.

The final countdown

If you read through your work again at this stage, you probably won't spot any more errors. After all, they've already survived one or two very thorough edits and several read-throughs. Yet these mistakes would stand out a mile if you were reading someone else's work.

So just before you post your work off to the publisher, print it out one more time for a final check. This final check should be a slow and painstaking one – and, ideally, be carried out by someone else.

Debugging your book

Here's an idea I've borrowed from the world of computer programming. In some software companies, programmers hand their work to a team of testers and give them a reward for every bug (mistake) they find. You could do the same with your book. Edit and polish it as best you can, then hand it over to your own team of testers – friends, family, colleagues, writing circle members, and so on. Give them a reward for each problem or mistake they find. The more they find, the more it'll cost you – and quite right too.

> 'Debugging' really does mean getting the bugs out. In the early days of computing when the machines filled entire rooms, moths and other creepy-crawlies sometimes got into the electrics, causing short-circuits and wrong answers. The debuggers job was to find and remove them. Thomas Edison also called minor problems with his inventions 'bugs'.

The next step

There's only one thing left to do now: get the book published as quickly as possible and make sure it sells. That's the subject of the next chapter.

19 The fastest ways to sell your book

And so we reach the final stage in our journey: getting your book into the hands of your many readers. And that means selling it. In fact, you should have been thinking about selling your book before you even started writing it.

Three options immediately spring to mind: find an agent, find a publisher, or self-publish it. But we're overlooking the easiest way of all: get someone else to do it all for you.

Marketing comes first

Marketing – because that's what selling your book is all about – is one of the first things you should think about when you come up with an idea for a book. Who would read such a book? Why would they want it? How will you let them know about it? How can you persuade them (or a publisher) to buy it?

This year we are mostly publishing...

You need to know what's being published at the moment and what's in and out of fashion. If it's not in fashion, no one will want it – especially publishers. Visit your local bookshop and check out the latest books. Get hold of publishers' latest catalogues to see what's popular. Write your book to fit that market – even if it means having to rethink your idea.

Who do you know?

Personal recommendation is one of the best ways to get an agent or publisher. It's also one of the fastest. (The best way of all is for an agent or publisher to come to you, but we'll cover that later.) With a personal recommendation, your book is more likely be read and seriously considered. If it's not suitable for them, they're more likely to tell you why, and perhaps suggest changes, or recommend other agents or publishers you should contact. Without a recommendation, your book will probably receive only a cursory glance, followed by a standard rejection slip that tells you little or nothing.

Your local writer's circle will probably have at least one published writer, who might be willing to put you in touch with his own agent or publisher and give a personal recommendation. If there are any other writing groups in your area, join those too. You never know who might be there, who they might know, who they might have as a guest speaker, and so on. If any of the groups have guest speakers, check the schedule for any publishers, agents and editors, and make sure you attend the meetings on those dates. It's not so much what they have to say – although that can be interesting and useful – it's the chance to chat with them afterwards. Tell them about yourself and your book, give them a business card and, if it's appropriate, arrange to make contact again in a few days time.

> A business card shows that you're a professional writer (even if you aren't) and can get you into all sorts of places. They're easy to make yourself, or any print and copy shop can make them for you. Keep them simple: no graphics, plain font, your name, occupation (writer, freelance journalist, or whatever you prefer) and your contact details.

Publisher seeks authors

Check magazines such as *Writers' News* for news about publishers and agents who are seeking new authors. Experienced editors or agents sometimes leave larger companies and set up on their own. Be ready to hit them with your submission. They'll probably have taken some high-profile clients with them, but they'll be eager to score a few more quick wins to help them get established. When you come across news items like this, get your query letter in the post the same day.

Who publishes a book like yours?

Visit your local bookshop and look for books that are similar to yours, and make a note of who publishes them. These publishers are the obvious choice when it comes to deciding who you're going to send your book to. When you contact them, mention the similarity between your book and those they've published.

It's not worth carrying out this check in the library. You need to see what's being published right now, and what's coming up in the next few months, not what was published a year or more ago. They might have stopped producing that type of book.

Marketing Plan

You can virtually guarantee your book will be published if you include an impressive marketing plan with your proposal or synopsis. Make sure you mention your marketing plan in your query letter too. You'll need to demonstrate that you have the ability, willingness, and connections to sell a guaranteed number of books yourself. And that means hundreds or thousands of books, not just a handful for your friends. The more sales you can guarantee, the better your chances of getting published.

How can you sell that many books?

- Advertise in newsletters or magazines you run or have a close association with.

- Perhaps a newspaper or magazine has agreed to produce a feature about you.

- Do you know a journalist or someone involved in television or radio who could get your book reviewed, or arrange for you to be interviewed?

- Clubs and other organisations might have expressed an interest in your book.

- You (or the publisher) might be able to advertise in specialist magazines – give details of the readership and likely number of sales.

- You might have an arrangement with your local bookshop to hold a book-signing session and feature your book in their window.

- Perhaps you teach – or could teach – a class, and could sell copies to your students.

- You could set up a stall at a relevant fair, festival, exhibition or convention, or share a stall with someone else.

- You could give talks at writer's circles, literary festivals, specialist clubs and associations, women's groups, and so on, and offer signed copies for sale at the end.

- Consider bulk sales to bookshops, gift shops, specialist shops, hotels and so on, especially if you've had some success in the past.

- Advertise or sell your book on your own website, or on someone else's.

It's worth reading a few books on marketing before you start putting your own plan together.

As well as listing the methods you'll use to sell all these books, you'll also have to say how many you expect to sell. How can you come up with these figures other than by pure guesswork?

Find people who have done this sort of thing before. How well did their books do? Find someone who's marketing their book right now. How are they marketing it? Look for adverts for books in magazines, or look for interviews with authors. If it states that you can buy a copy direct from the author, make contact with them. Exchange marketing tips, and see if you can sell a few copies of their book on their behalf. How easy or difficult is it?

Magazine advertising departments should be able to tell you how many readers they have, and their age range and social class – especially if you pretend to be a potential advertiser. What percentage of the magazine's readership would buy your book?

You'll need to come up with hard evidence to convince the publisher to accept your proposal. But if you can guarantee a certain number of sales, and that number is higher than their break-even point, *and* your book really is good enough for publication, then published it will be.

And it's not just a case of getting your book published. As a first-time writer, your publisher won't put nearly as much effort into marketing your book as you would like. If you want it to be a major success, it's down to you.

See if you can do at least one thing every day to help market your book: send out press releases, contact bookshops and website owners, arrange to give talks, and so on.

The title and front cover

Glance along a shelf of books. How long do your eyes focus on each one? A second? Maybe less? What about when you see one that interests you? How long do you look at its title before deciding whether to pick it up? Three or four seconds? That's how long you have to sell your book.

Spend some time in a bookshop looking at the titles. Why do certain titles catch your eye? Try to come up with a title for your book that's equally eye-catching. It needs to tell your readers exactly what your book is all about. It also needs to sell it to them. A non-fiction book's title should promise them a solution to their problems, or guarantee the results they will achieve. A novel's title should indicate what sort of story the book contains – and it should promise great entertainment.

If you have any control over the cover design, make sure it fits in with the emotional effect you want to achieve. Choose colours, fonts and images to emphasise that effect. Consider adding a sub-title to explain exactly what the book is all about.

The back cover, blurb and quotes

The back cover is where you really exercise your powers of persuasion. In the case of a non-fiction book, it might resemble the query letter you sent to the publisher. Begin with a sentence or two to explain the need for the book. Then show how your book fills that need – summarise the features and benefits. End with a section about you, your experience and qualifications, showing why you're the best person to write this book. You only have 100 – 150 words to hook your reader and fill him with desire.

In the case of a novel, the back cover usually begins by stating the opening dilemma the main character faces. The next section acts like a trailer for a movie: a few exciting highlights and plenty of unanswered questions that leave your reader anxious to find out what happens.

How about adding a quote or two to help with marketing? If you look closely at the back covers of some published books you'll see that the quotes often refer to an entirely different book. Sometimes it's simply 'praise' for the writer and doesn't relate to a book at all. You could do this too. Perhaps a celebrity judge praised your writing ability in a short story competition. Maybe a well-known writer was your tutor on a writing course and wrote a nice comment about your work.

There's considerable debate about how much difference celebrity quotes actually make. But if you can get a good one then use it; it certainly can't hurt, and it might help to sell a few more books.

How to write query letters, proposals and synopses

This topic alone could fill an entire book – and there are several very good ones available. A good book will show you the best ways of obtaining all the information you need, how to lay it out correctly, and how to write it in such a way that it will be hard to turn down.

A proposal should not only describe the book itself, but its place in the market. You'll need to list any competing titles and state why yours is better. You'll need to accurately estimate the size of the market. You'll need to state your expertise and background – what makes you the perfect person to write this book? You'll need to state what marketing and promotion you can provide – see the marketing section above. There's more about writing query letters, proposals and synopses later in the chapter.

> Don't forget: if marketing isn't for you and you can trust someone else to do it for you, hand your book over to them and get on with writing the next one. Teamwork saves time.

Don't give up

Many writers send their work to only three or four publishers or agents, get rejected, and then give up. If you really want to be published, you need to be prepared to send your work to twenty or more companies. Make a list of all the people you could send it to. Then, as it comes back from one, send it straight off to the next one on the list. This saves a lot of anxiety and depression.

After ten rejections, consider whether you need to make any changes to your query letter, proposal, synopsis, or the book itself, taking into account any feedback you've received. But carry on sending it out. When you've completely exhausted your list, you can assume there's no interest in this sort of book at the moment. File it away and concentrate on your next one.

When you do eventually get a book accepted, dig out the rejected ones and show them to the person who has just accepted your latest book. They might well be interested in them now, even if they rejected them previously. At the very least, they should be able to tell you what you need to do to make them publishable.

We want your book

When a publisher accepts your book for publication, they issue you with a contract. It's a good idea to get someone who understands these things to go through it to make sure you're getting a fair payment and you aren't signing away all the rights.

Don't choose your local solicitor. He probably won't understand publishing contracts and he'll just waste time quibbling over tiny details that are standard practice throughout the industry. A better idea would be to get the Society of Authors to check it for you. You'll need to join as an associate member, and you can only do this if you've had a book accepted for publication. Once it's been published, you can upgrade to full membership and receive other benefits.

My friend who works in publishing

See if you can make friends with someone who works for a publishing company or literary agency. He doesn't have to be an editor or agent. He could be a salesperson, secretary, typist or even the cleaner. The important thing is that he'll know the editors and agents and be able to make an approach on your behalf. If he's as excited about your book as you are then he should do a good job of selling it for you. Give him a copy of the manuscript to take into work with him – and make sure it's not your only copy.

Why isn't it a bestseller?

If your publisher doesn't seem to be making much of an effort to promote your book, or if you're self-publishing it, contact a public relations or marketing company. They will *definitely* be willing to promote your book for you. The real question is whether you think they'll make a good job of it. Will you sell enough extra books to cover their fee?

Even if you barely cover their fee, it might still have been a worthwhile campaign if they managed to arrange TV and radio interviews and get newspaper coverage. That will be extremely useful when it comes to selling your next book. More people will have heard of you, and many will consider you an expert in your subject, even if they didn't buy your first book.

Nobody knows who I am

You can also use your own writing skills to become better known. Describe how you came to write your book. Tell how your fascination with the story or the subject compelled you to write about it. Talk about the problems you encountered: the setbacks, the dead ends, the problems you had finding the time to write, the near impossibility of finding a quiet place to write, how you scraped enough money together for the books, courses and equipment you needed. Talk about how you managed to finish the book in spite of all the things people have said about you – how you could never finish anything, how you'd never amount to anything, and so on. Every book is a struggle to write and every writer has a story to tell about themselves and that book.

This piece of writing shouldn't be more than two pages long, and if you can get it all on a single page that's even better. What you've just written will become a press release. You'll find plenty of information on how to write a press release on the internet, and there are books dedicated to the subject. The main factor that will decide whether the media uses your story is how newsworthy it is.

> Always address your press release to specific people by name rather than putting 'The Editor' or 'Dear Sir'. This will make a significant difference to the success of your campaign. Don't think that it doesn't matter. It does.

Send your press release to everyone you can think of: TV and radio stations, newspapers, magazines, websites, and so on. Make sure you've included your contact details, because if the story really takes off you'll be getting a lot of phone calls. It doesn't matter if you don't have a publisher for your book yet. If you can attract enough attention, publishers will ask to see it. Make sure you're ready for them.

The combination trick

One of the main reasons why publishers turn books down is that they don't think they can sell enough copies. But how about combining traditional publishing and self-publishing by offering to buy a certain number from them – say 500 or 1,000 – at cost price? That should make them sit up and take notice. Your book must be of publishable standard of course. And there needs to be a market for it, so both you and the publisher can be reasonably sure of selling your stock.

The benefits are enormous: you'll have the credibility of being published by a recognised 'brand', professional editing and design, a nationwide marketing campaign, national distribution, and so on. You're also more likely to get your book reviewed in the press – many newspapers won't review self-published books (we'll look at how to get around that problem later).

Even if you barely sell enough books to cover your costs, it will still have been worth doing. Your book got published after all – and the next one should do much better.

> I highly recommend the following books: *Marketing Your Book: An Author's Guide* by Alison Baverstock. *An Author's guide to Publishing* by Michael Legat. *How to get published and make a lot of money* by Susan Page.

Other formats

You can reuse the text of your book in many ways, creating spin-off products and making even more money for very little extra work.

Audio books

Audio books are becoming increasingly popular. People listen to books while travelling, gardening, doing the housework, exercising, walking, and much more. Digital audio players such as Apple's iPod are selling in huge numbers – and you can use them for more than just music. To make an audio version of your book, all you need to do is read it aloud, or find someone with a good reading voice, then record it. It helps if you have a computer with a CD writer and some audio-editing software, such as Audacity (see Resources), so you can remove any glitches. If you plan to sell a lot of copies, it'll be more cost effective to have them professionally duplicated rather than making them yourself. Companies who offer this service advertise widely in most music magazines. Bear in mind that you'll probably need three or four CDs to cover the whole book.

Giving talks

I've already mentioned giving talks, lectures and presentations as a way of selling your book. You could base your talk on the book itself. You could also charge an entrance fee. The more valuable people perceive the information to be, the higher the fee you can charge. And you can sell them a copy of the book at the end. Or increase the entrance fee to include the cost of the book, and give everyone a 'free' copy.

Videos and DVDs

While you're giving your talk, get someone to video it for you. You can then sell the video recording of your talk. Video editing can easily be done on home computers these days, and the equipment is affordable and widely available. If you don't fancy doing it yourself, you shouldn't have to look too far to find someone who can do it for you.

Short stories and articles

You can break your book into a number of short stories or articles which can be sold to magazines or given away free to promote your book. A published book is a fantastic demonstration of your writing ability and knowledge. That could lead to a regular column in a newspaper or magazine, or you might join the group of 'preferred writers' who are specially commissioned by editors to write features on specific subjects or themes.

Other rights

You (or your agent) might be able to sell the serial rights to your book to a newspaper, as well as foreign and film rights.

Consultancy and tuition

A published non-fiction book confers expert status on you. You can offer coaching and consultancy services on the subject and command high fees.

If your novel has been published, you can offer yourself as a guest speaker or writing tutor and visit writing circles, literary festivals, writing courses, and so on. As well as being paid for your services, these are great opportunities to sell your books.

Fiction

What is it?

Publishers are reluctant to consider any novel that doesn't have an obvious genre. Romance: yes, horror: yes, science fiction and fantasy: yes. But if you've written a gothic horror western romantic comedy crime adventure in space and all the characters are robots, well, there aren't many publishers who would touch it. There's no obvious market and no obvious shelf in the bookshops. Maybe when you're famous you could try the mix-and-match groundbreaking stuff, but even then there's no guarantee your publisher will want it.

Competitions

Enter your novel for as many competitions and awards for unpublished novels as you can find. Enter as many short story competitions as you can too. You may be a novelist at heart, but there are a lot more short story competitions than novel competitions, and they're a great way of getting noticed. Even if you're only a runner-up or shortlisted in a competition, it's worth mentioning in your query letters.

Multi-book deals

If you've only written one novel and have no immediate plans to write another, publishers might not be quite as interested as you might expect. Publishers generally aren't looking for one-off novels and single book deals. If they've decided to invest in a new writer, it's because they believe they have future potential. Your first book probably won't sell very well, but they accept that; it takes time to become known. Your second book will sell more, and their marketing department will give it more of a push. Your third book will sell even more. As your name becomes known, demand also grows for reprints of your earlier work – and those original first editions become worth a lot of money.

   You often hear of new writers being offered two-book or three-book deals. Now you know why. It's always best to have plans in place for a second novel, or even a third. It doesn't have to be more than a germ of an idea at this stage. Mention it in your query letter, and perhaps include a mini-synopsis if you've thought that far ahead (half a page will be enough). You'll be doing yourself a massive favour.

Agents

Many publishers now say they'll only accept submissions via an agent, so approaching publishers directly is generally a waste of time. It's better to concentrate on finding a good agent. Although they take a percentage of your earnings – up to fifteen percent – they can usually get you a bigger advance and a better royalty rate than you would be able to negotiate yourself.

Your agent will usually shield you from rejection letters, collect money owed to you, and sometimes provide creative and editorial advice. But how do you get one?

Getting an agent

The best method I've come across (apart from personal recommend-ation) is the one given in Susan Page's book *How to get published and make a lot of money*. You really ought to buy this book and memorise every word. Here's a very brief summary of Susan's method for getting an agent:

1. Make a list of all suitable agents (not publishers) – see below.

2. Send query letters to all of them simultaneously.

3. Of those who ask to see the book (or the proposal, synopsis, or sample chapters) send it to them *one at a time*. Don't send it to the next one until the previous one has said yes or no.

4. If six weeks pass without a response, contact the agent and politely ask how soon you might expect a decision.

5. Give the agent another two weeks and then call again. If there's still no news, decide whether to wait or move on to the next agent. If you really want that particular agent, wait a little longer.

6. If you want to move on to the next agent, write to the agent who currently has the book. Tell him (politely) that another agent has expressed an interest and unless you receive a response within seven days you'll allow him to see it.

7. If there's still no response, send the book to the next agent who expressed an interest.

Finding an agent

Agents are listed in many places. *The Writers' and Artist's Yearbook, The Writer's Handbook, Publishing News,* and *The Bookseller* are all good starting points. You'll often find news about the latest publishing deals in writing magazines, and these often give details of the agent. Reputable agents should be listed on the Association of Authors' Agents website (www.agentsassoc.co.uk). You can also find a list of most UK and US agents at the Everyone Who's Anyone website (http://everyonewhosanyone.com).

Agents, like publishers, tend to specialise in a certain type of book. There's no point sending your romantic comedy to an agent who's only interested in science fiction and fantasy, so you'll need to do a little more research here. The agent listings above should state which genres each agent specialises in.

If your book is similar to another author's and you'd like his agent to look at your book, contact the Book Trust to find out who represents him. Or check inside the book and see if he mentions his agent in the dedication or acknowledgement. If all else fails, phone the publisher and ask who the agent is. If they seem reluctant, tell them you're interested in optioning the movie rights to the book in question. It's a sneaky trick, but it usually works.

The query letter

Despite what everyone seems to think, a query letter is perfectly straightforward and easy to write. It's just a standard one-page letter. Be sure to address it to an individual agent by name. If you don't know his name, phone the agency and ask who would be the best person to represent a book like yours.

Divide the main text into four paragraphs as follows:

1. All about you – who you are and why you're passionate about this particular story.

2. All about the book – the genre, number of characters, word count (to the nearest 5,000), and an overview of the storyline.

3. State that you've read and enjoyed some of their previous publications, and mention the titles and authors of one or two of them that are roughly similar to your own book. Also mention that you've looked at their latest catalogue and feel that your book would fit well on their current list.

4. Additional information – writing competitions you've won or been shortlisted for, previous publishing experience, marketing ideas (be brief), and any other relevant information. Agents, like publishers, are looking for long-term writers, so make sure you put something in this section about your next book – preferably one in the same genre. You only need a one-line description at this stage.

The synopsis

Personally, I would always include a brief synopsis with the query letter and offer to send a full synopsis if the agent is interested. The brief synopsis should be no more than two pages, with the events of each chapter summarised in one or two sentences. If the agent is interested, he will ask to see a full synopsis, a full synopsis plus two or three completed chapters, or the whole book.

As with the query letter, a lot of mystery seems to surround the synopsis, but it's a perfectly straightforward document. However, the success of your book could depend on the quality of the synopsis, so it's worth spending a good deal of time making it perfect.

The full synopsis is a condensed version of the whole story – yes, you do have to reveal the ending. A good rule of thumb is to make it 1/25 the length of the novel, so if your novel is 250 pages your synopsis should be around ten pages. Condense each chapter or major scene into a single paragraph, but *don't* use chapter headings (chapter 1, chapter 2, and so on). Use the present tense: 'Stan Bean thinks his wife Mavis is having an affair', not 'Stan Bean thought his wife Mavis was having an affair'.

Don't simply list the events that happen in the story. You need to make it sound exciting and include plenty of emotion – the stronger the better.

Here's an extract from a bad synopsis: 'Stan Bean's neighbour Frank Harrolds killed Stan's cat, so Stan kidnapped Frank's wife.'

And here's an improved version: 'Devastated by the death of his beloved cat, Stan Bean drinks himself into a fierce rage and swears revenge on his neighbour Frank Harrolds, who killed the cat when he caught it digging up his prize-winning roses. Stan rips his shotgun from its wall-mounting, storms over to Frank's house, breaks down the door with a single blow, and drags Frank's wife Sarah screaming from her bed.'

Maybe you could do a better job, but my point is that the first version is so dull and lifeless it's more likely to send the agent to sleep than persuade him to take you on as a client. The second version should make him want to read on to the end to find out what happens – and then ask to see the whole book.

Non-fiction

Most non-fiction writers don't have an agent, but work directly with publishers. Non-fiction query letters and proposals are also quite different from the query letters and synopses a novelist writes.

The query letter

This is a one-page business letter addressed to a specific editor at a publishing company. If you don't know the editor's name, phone the publisher and ask which editor would be the best person to contact about a book on your specialist subject. Divide a non-fiction query letter into four paragraphs, as follows:

1. What problem does your book address? How did you spot a gap in the market? If you realised the extent of the problem after conducting or reading about a survey, give the details here.

2. A description of your book and how it addresses the problem. What will people learn or be able to do as a result of reading your book?

3. Who is the book aimed at? What market is there for a book of this type? Does it fit into an existing series? If other books on this subject are already available, how does yours fit into the market or improve on competing titles?

4. All about you – why you are the obvious person to write this book, your qualifications and experience in this subject, relevant organisations you belong to, previous writing or publishing experience. Also mention anything that would help with marketing.

The proposal

As with novels, I would always include a brief outline of the proposed book with the query letter. This should be no more than two pages and will summarise each chapter in one or two sentences. Mention this outline in the query letter and offer to send a full proposal.

A non-fiction proposal is usually a simple one-paragraph-per-chapter outline. I recommend reading a book on writing non-fiction book proposals so you make a good job of writing yours. The proposal is what will sell your book to the publisher, because, unlike a novel, your book doesn't exist yet. You won't start writing it until you've agreed the format with the publisher, although he might ask you to prepare a sample chapter to give him an idea of what the finished book might look like.

Your expertise

One of the main reasons why non-fiction proposals are rejected is because you aren't enough of an expert in your subject, based on what you said in your query letter.

If you do have the expertise then your query letter just needs pepping up a bit. If you don't have the expertise then you must acquire it. This might take some time of course, but it's essential if you want to be taken seriously. Remember my definition of an expert from earlier: if you don't think you're capable of teaching an evening class in your subject then you shouldn't be writing a book about it.

A quicker alternative is to find an expert or recognised authority in the subject. Either collaborate with him, or get him to write a supporting statement saying he's reviewed your book and thinks it's worthy of publication.

Self-publishing

A licence to print money?

Self-publishing is not a cheap option, and certainly isn't for everyone. Make sure you've accounted for all the costs before you set your cover price – unless you're willing to make a loss.

You'll need to take into account the artwork, design, layout and typesetting, ISBN number and barcode, as well as the printing, marketing and distribution costs.

If it costs you £3.00 to print each book and your cover price is £10.00, that's a healthy profit of £7.00 per book – in theory. But if you sell it through a bookshop, they'll want a forty percent discount. They'll pay you £6.00 per copy, leaving you £3.00 profit. If you sell it through a distributor, they'll take fifty-five percent. You'll get £4.50 per book and make just £1.50 profit.

Another marketing plan

Earlier, we looked at creating a marketing plan to sell your book to publishers. If you're planning to self-publish your book then you need a marketing plan for that too.

Your plan should include all your marketing ideas, plus goals and milestones so you can measure your success. You'll find lots of good ideas in John Kremer's book *1001 Ways to Market Your Books*.

Don't stop marketing your book after a few weeks; it'll take much longer than that for it to become established. It'll probably take a full year before your marketing efforts show any real results. And most of the marketing experts I've spoken to recommend that you should continue marketing your book for three years.

To make the most money, forget about bookshops. You'll need to sell your books yourself – through a website, talks and lectures, magazine adverts, posters, TV and radio interviews, newspaper articles, and anything else you can think of. Don't forget to take your storage, advertising and travelling costs into account.

Get plenty of quotes

Get several quotes for each aspect of your book's production. Printing costs, for example, depend on the dimensions of the book, the quality of the paper, the number of pages, the type of cover and binding, the need for colour, and so on. The price will also vary depending on the number of copies you need – the more you have printed, the cheaper each book will be. You need to find the right balance between quality, quantity and price, but you'll undoubtedly have to make some compromises.

Selling via a website

Consider setting up a website for your book so you can take orders online – or at least give a postal address so people can send you orders. Include some additional marketing material such as sample text and images. You could also have a section for readers' feedback and questions.

Try to get other websites to add a link to yours or include a review of your book. Do the same for them in return.

Your website could also feature other books on the same subject. Most online bookshops operate an affiliates or associates scheme. You feature their books on your website and they process the orders for you and pay you a small fee for every book sold.

Newspaper and magazine reviews

Newspapers hardly ever review self-published books. That's unfortunate because a good review is a great way of bringing your book to the public's attention. However, there are a few tricks that should help you get around this problem.

> Try sending a few free copies of your book to newspapers, magazines and radio stations to give away as competition prizes. That should earn you a mention.

As I mentioned earlier, your local newspaper(s) will undoubtedly be interested in your book, regardless of how it was published, so send them a press release to tell them about it.

Another useful trick is to send newspapers and magazines an extract from your book that they can print. When they print this free extract, they'll also print the details about your book of course. This is actually better than a review because you have complete control over what they print – and they can't give you a bad review!

Writing magazines such as *Writing Magazine*, *Writers' News* and *Writer's Forum* will usually be quite happy to give your self-published

> It can cost several hundred pounds to place an advert in a magazine. Each review should generate at least as many sales as an advert without costing you anything. So I would always send a free copy of the book to *every* magazine that covers the subject – so long as they have a book review section or mention them in their news pages.

book a mention, especially if you're a subscriber. Specialist magazines that cover your subject will usually review it too, so send them a press release and a free copy. If there are too many magazines for this to be economical, just send a press release. You won't get a full review of course, but most of them will give your book a mention and tell their readers where they can get it from.

Selling on location

If your book is about (or set in) a particular location, go along there and set up a nice display of your books. And keep going back until you've sold them all. If it sells out quickly, get some more printed and go back as soon as possible.

> You'll need a licence to trade in some places, so make sure you check on this before setting up your stall.

This can work particularly well if you've chosen a popular tourist resort. People are much more willing to part with their cash on holiday, and your book will make a good souvenir. Make sure you also have some leaflets (including an order form) to give to people who don't have enough money with them. The more tourists a place gets, the more books you'll sell, so you might like to plan your book with this in mind.

This can be an extremely pleasurable way of spending the summer. You can spend the winter at home writing the next volume and living off your profits. Next summer, take along copies of your old book as well as your new one – some people will buy both.

Not just bookshops

Don't restrict yourself to selling your book through bookshops. Most people never go in bookshops anyway. See if you can find other shops that are appropriate to the subject of your book, and ask them to put a few copies on display on a sale or return basis. Agree to take back any

When you get your book printed, see if the printer will run off a few poster-size enlargements of the cover. Alternatively, your local print and copy shop should be able to produce them for you.

unsold copies after a specified period – the end of the tourist season perhaps. Give them some leaflets, and maybe a poster to display too. Go to neighbouring towns as well as your own. Also try hotels, gift shops, post offices, stately homes, and anywhere else where visitors are likely to pass through in large numbers.

You might go on selling your book steadily over a number of years, ordering occasional reprints from the printer, and perhaps issuing a revised edition every couple of years.

Market research – before writing

Before you even write one word of your book, visit some of the places where you hope to sell your book and ask people for their opinion. What do they think of your idea for a book? Would they buy it? Would they stock it? Do they think it would do well? How many copies do they think they could sell? What do they think of the price – does it sound like good value? Show them a brief outline of the proposed book. Do they think it covers the subject fully? Can they suggest any changes?

This will give you a rough idea of how successful your book is likely to be and, if you decide to proceed, how many copies you'll need to get printed.

Your friendly neighbourhood bookshop

How well do you know the manager and staff in your local bookshop? It pays to get to know them because they can help your career enormously. For example, how about if the shop dedicated its entire window display to your book for a week? Or perhaps they could display a photo of you in the window next to a copy of your book and a sign saying 'local author'. They might arrange signing sessions too.

Print on demand (POD)

Print on demand has revolutionised self-publishing. Your book is stored on the company's computer. Whenever you need a copy, the computer prints one on a high-speed printer. A full-colour cover is printed separately. The cover and insides are then loaded into a binding machine which glues it all together. The result: a standard paperback book.

Print on demand companies charge a set-up fee for processing your book and storing it on their computer. This fee varies between companies, so it's worth comparing them. They also charge a printing cost for each book –

> Remember to take the set-up fee into account as well as the printing and postage costs.

usually about a penny per page plus fifty or sixty pence for the cover, so a standard paperback book will cost £2.50 – £3.00. You'll also have to pay the postage costs to have the books sent to you. And there's a small annual maintenance charge if they continue to store your book on their system.

It costs more to print books using this process, but it offers significant advantages over traditional printing. For example, if you have no idea how many books you can sell, it doesn't matter; simply order them singly or in small batches as you need them. You

> It's best to order books in batches of about fifty, which should all fit in a single box. Order another box when your stock runs low.

don't have to pay a huge lump sum to have thousands of copies printed, and nor do you have to find somewhere to store them. And so long as you keep paying the annual maintenance charge, your book never goes out of print.

The main advantage of print on demand is that it doesn't matter if your book doesn't sell very well. It's a great way of testing the market for the sort of books you write. If one fails to sell, write another one and try again.

If your books start selling in large numbers, it's probably worth switching to traditional litho printing. The cost per book will be significantly lower, but the whole lot will be printed in one go, so you'll have to find somewhere to store them.

I've listed several UK print on demand companies below. It's worth contacting each of them and asking for a copy of their print on demand guide so you can compare their services and prices.

Anthony Rowe Ltd
2 Whittle Drive, Highfield Industrial Estate, Eastbourne, East Sussex, BN23 6QH
Tel: 01323 500040
email: bob.hunt@antonyrowe.co.uk
Website: www.anthonyrowe.co.uk

AuthorHouse
PO Box 7295, Milton Keynes, MK13 8YJ
Tel: 0800 1974150
email: use enquiry form on website
Website: www.authorhouse.co.uk

The Better Book Company
Warblington Lodge, The Gardens, Havant, Hampshire, PO9 2XH
Tel: 023 9248 1160
email: editors@better-book.co.uk
Website: www.better-book.co.uk

Pen Press
39 Chesham Road, Brighton, BN2 1NB
Tel: 0845 1080 530
email: info@penpress.net
Website: www.penpress.net

Trafford Publishing
Enterprise House, Wistaston Road Business Centre, Crewe, CW2 7RP
Tel: 0845 230 9601 ext 8063
email: info.uk@trafford.com
Website: www.trafford.com/8063

Preparing your book for print on demand

Your book probably exists as several word processing files at the moment. Print on demand companies can turn these files into a book for you, but you'll have to pay for the typesetting and layout work. You can save money by doing this yourself.

You'll need to lay out the book exactly as you want it to appear, using the exact page dimensions supplied by the company. Don't forget the preliminary pages, plus the table of contents and index if you're producing a non-fiction book. You probably won't be able to do all this with your word processor.

Professional desktop publishing packages include Adobe Page-Maker, Adobe InDesign, and Quark Xpress, but these cost several hundred pounds. Programs such as Microsoft Publisher and Serif PagePlus will do the job for a fraction of the cost.

Most print on demand companies work with PDF (Portable Document Format) files. The latest version of PagePlus exports files in this format, but they might not be fully compatible with the print on

I bought all the software I needed on eBay for a fraction of the normal retail price. If you do this, make sure you're buying the real thing, not pirate copies or backups. Look out for those that say they're *new, sealed* and *unregistered.*

demand company's system, so you'll need to check this with them. If the files aren't acceptable, you'll need to use Adobe Acrobat to generate them.

Most companies also have a basic set of pre-prepared cover designs, for which there's usually little or no charge. However, you'll probably want to design your own cover, and that means you'll need a graphics package such as Jasc Paint Shop Pro, Macromedia Fireworks or Adobe Photoshop.

Setting yourself up for print on demand publishing isn't cheap, but once you've bought the software you can use it over and over again for future books.

For this book, I used Microsoft Word 2000 to write the text and Macromedia Fireworks 4 and Adobe Photoshop 6 for the graphics, including the cover. I used Serif PagePlus 10 for the design and layout, and exported the finished book to PDF using Adobe Acrobat 6 Professional.

Selling your self-published book online

Amazon Advantage

To get Amazon to stock your book, go to their website and sign up for Amazon Advantage. The process is very simple. The big drawback is the cost. Amazon charges a sixty percent fee for stocking your book, so you'll

> Amazon's fee is reduced to fifty-five percent if you sell more than £50,000 worth of books in a year.

only receive forty percent of the selling price. But there's a catch: Amazon decides the selling price, not you. And you have to send each batch of books to their warehouse at your own expense.

Let's return to the sums from earlier. If it costs £3.00 to print each book and the cover price is £10.00, Amazon gives you £4.00 per copy, leaving £1.00 profit – but it'll probably cost you at least that much to send it to their warehouse, so you won't make a penny. However, if they decide to knock thirty percent off and sell it for £7.00, you'll only receive £2.80 – a *loss* of £0.20 per copy before you even consider the postage costs. You'll need to set your cover price much higher, or reduce costs by using traditional printing rather than print on demand.

eBooks

Sales of eBooks are beginning to take off. They don't take up any space, there are no printing costs, and increasing numbers of people carry handheld computers with built-in eBook readers.

The majority of eBooks are PDF files. Until recently, you needed Adobe Acrobat to create these, but several companies now produce much cheaper packages – and even give them away free on the CDs that come with computer magazines.

People who buy your eBook in this format will need a copy of Adobe Reader on their computer. Most people already have this, and it can be downloaded free of charge from Adobe's website (www.adobe.com).

Another popular eBook format is Microsoft Reader, which is pre-installed on many handheld computers. To produce files in this format you'll need Microsoft Word and a free add-in that you can download from Microsoft's website (www.microsoft.com).

Many people prefer short eBooks because they're more comfortable to read on a screen than longer ones, so consider splitting your book into a number of shorter eBooks and selling them for a reduced fee – although the combined price for the complete set might come to more than the price of the original book.

You might also consider writing shorter books specifically for the eBook market. They'll be much faster to write, so as soon as you spot the need for such a book, you can put it together quickly and get it on sale while there's plenty of interest.

> If you've written a short eBook, consider calling it a *report* or *manual* rather than a book. Most people will pay a lot more for a report or manual than for a book. The important point is that buyers must perceive it as being good value for money.

Selling eBooks

Amazon sells eBooks as well as the printed variety. You can also sell eBooks direct from your own website. With a little technical knowledge this can be completely automated so the website collects payments and sends out eBooks without you having to do anything.

ClickBank

A great way to sell eBooks is to use ClickBank (www.clickbank.com), which specialises in selling eBooks. Customers browse ClickBank, find the book they need, enter their payment details, and then download the book immediately. ClickBank handles the payments and pays the money into your bank account.

You'll have to pay a set-up fee of $49.95, then $1 + 7.5% for each book you sell. Since you don't have to pay any printing costs, you could reduce the price of your eBook to £7.00. After deducting ClickBank's fee, you'll receive about £5.90 per copy.

eBay

Another very popular way of selling books – printed and eBooks – is through eBay. To get started, visit their website (www.ebay.co.uk) and click on 'How to sell an item'. This will tell you everything you need to know.

> It's important to choose the right category to list your book in on eBay. If you get it wrong, nobody will find it and you won't sell any copies at all.

If you have several different eBooks for sale, you could also set up your own shop on eBay. Again, you'll find full details on their website.

I believe it will sell

In earlier chapters, I talked about having a positive approach and believing in yourself, reinforcing the positive thoughts and blocking out the negative ones.

Close your eyes and visualise your book on sale, with long queues of people waiting to buy it. See it sitting at the top of the bestseller lists. See and hear yourself giving successful talks and signing lots of copies afterwards. See and hear yourself on TV talking about your book and everything going well. Imagine the fantastic reviews your book receives. Think of a specific amount of money you want to make from your book. Visualise that amount sitting in your bank account. What will you spend it on? Visualise those things for a few minutes. How will your lifestyle change? Picture yourself living that lifestyle: the sights, the sounds, the smells, the feeling of living your life the way you want to.

When you've done that for a few minutes, open your eyes and you'll probably feel great, excited, ready to get out there and sell your book. Repeat this exercise every day for several weeks. Eventually your brain will believe it's true. And if you think you're successful, then you will be successful.

20 Conclusion

As you've seen, writing a book needn't take up a huge chunk of your life. And if the book really matters to you, you'll make time to write it rather than waiting for enough free time to come along.

Writing a book quickly has many advantages. For example, if you spot a gap in the market you can fill it almost immediately. The techniques in this book should allow you to get your book into the hands of those readers well before anyone else does. Another advantage is that you don't have time to get bored.

Modern technology makes you far more effective and efficient, allowing you to research, plan and write at far greater speeds than ever before. When you combine new technology with the techniques used by writers of the past, it becomes possible for just about anyone to produce great books at a phenomenal rate. Recent innovations such as print on demand and eBooks allow you to get those books to your readers in a fraction of the time that traditional publishing takes, while eliminating most of the risks.

I'd like to leave you with these thoughts on being a successful writer:

1. Never write books just to make money. If you're a natural born writer then you have to write; you have no choice. If you have a wealth of knowledge that you'd like to share with the world then by all means share it, but the emphasis should be on the sharing rather than the selling. That doesn't mean you can't make a very good living out of it though.

2. Unless you're writing purely for pleasure, you should aim to sell every book you write. You should also feel confident that you will sell it, and – most importantly – feel proud to have written it.

3. Always strive to give *great* value for money rather than just good value for money. Try to pack in as much information and/or entertainment as possible. And then go the extra mile by including bonuses, as I've done with this book.

4. If there are similar books on the market, always identify what their shortcomings are. Make sure you know exactly how and why your book will be better than every one of those other books *before* you start writing it. If you don't think your book will be better, don't write it.

5. Strive for professionalism and quality at all times. With each book you write, you'll get a little better at it, but you'll never be quite as good a writer as you really want to be. Always write the best book you're capable of writing at that time, even if it takes a little longer.

Here's to your success!

Dave Haslett
Email: dave@ideas4writers.co.uk

Visit this book's website at: www.ideas4writers.co.uk/books
for updates and corrections, reviews, readers' feedback and more.

Appendix A   Resources

All trademarks acknowledged.
Prices correct at time of publication.

For updates see: www.ideas4writers.co.uk/books

Chapter 1

National Novel Writing Month (NaNoWriMo) – every November
www.nanowrimo.org

International 3-day novel writing contest – every September
www.3daynovel.com

Dave Fox's experience of entering the 3-day novel writing contest:
www.salon.com/books/feature/1999/11/16/threeday/index.html

Chapter 3

Healthy computing
setting up and using computer equipment correctly
www.healthycomputing.com

New World Music Ltd – natural sound recordings
Harmony House, Hillside Road East, Bungay, Suffolk NR35 8RX
Tel: 01986 891600
Email: Use enquiry form on website
Website: www.newworldmusic.com/uk/index.php

Mastery – The keys to success and long-term fulfilment
by George Leonard
ISBN: 0452267560
Published by: Penguin (1992)
Price (Amazon.co.uk): £4.25

Chapter 4

Dream Direct – software, computer accessories, video games, and collections of art and clip-art on CD-Rom
Website: www.edream.co.uk

Chapter 5

MindJet MindManager – software for creating Mind Maps
Website: www.mindjet.com

BrainStorm – multi-purpose thought assistant
Website: www.brainstormsw.com

The Mind Map Book
by Tony & Barry Buzan
ISBN: 0563487011
Published by: BBC Books (2003)
Price (Amazon.co.uk): £4.79

Chapter 6

Internet search engines:

AltaVista: www.altavista.co.uk
Ask Jeeves: www.ask.co.uk
DMOZ Open Directory Project: www.dmoz.org
Google: www.google.co.uk
MSN: search.msn.co.uk
WebCrawler: www.webcrawler.com
WebFetch: www.webfetch.com

Blogger – create your own web log and read other people's
www.blogger.com

The British Library
96 Euston Road, London, NW1 2DB
Tel: 020 7412 7609
Email: reader-services-enquiries@bl.uk
Website: www.bl.uk

The Speed Reading Book
by Tony Buzan
ISBN: 056348702X
Published by: BBC Books (2003)
Price (Amazon.co.uk): £4.79

Interviewing for Journalists
by Sally Adams & Wynford Hicks
ISBN: 0415229146
Published by: Routledge (2001)
Price (Amazon.co.uk): £10.99

Interviewing Techniques for Writers and Researchers
By Susan Dunne
ISBN: 0713641924
Published by A & C Black (1995)
Price (Amazon.co.uk): £4.75

The Sealed Knot – English Civil War Re-enactment
P.O. Box 2000, Nottingham, NG2 5LH
Email: info@sealedknot.org
Website: www.sealedknot.org

The Open University – TV schedule
www.open2.net

Research for Writers
by Ann Hoffmann
ISBN: 0713665769
Published by: A & C Black (2003)
Price (Amazon.co.uk): £9.79

Chapter 7

Treepad Lite – freeware outliner and organiser
www.treepad.com

Chapter 8

BBC News
Website: news.bbc.co.uk

Chapter 10

Dragon NaturallySpeaking – dictation software
www.scansoft.co.uk/naturallyspeaking

Chapter 11

Building a Character
by Konstantin Stanislavsky
ISBN: 0878309829
Published by: Routledge (2002)
Price (Amazon.co.uk): £22.08

The Creative Writing Coursebook
edited by Julia Bell & Andrew Magrs
ISBN: 0333782259
Published by: Pan (2001)
Price (Amazon.co.uk): £10.49

Hero with a Thousand Faces
by Joseph Campbell
ISBN: 0586085718
Published by: Fontana Press (1993)
Price (Amazon.co.uk): £6.99

Novel Writing - 16 Steps to Success
by Evan Marshall
ISBN: 0713668520
Published by: A & C Black (2004)
Price (Amazon.co.uk): £9.09

Chapter 13

EasyScript/ComputerScript
www.easyscript.com
    Prices (Amazon.co.uk):
    EasyScript Express: £15.39
    EasyScript I: £23.42 (with ComputerScript £120.50)
    EasyScript II: £46.85 (with ComputerScript £155.50)
    EasyScript III: £120.99 (with ComputerScript £172.50)

IntelliEdit and IntelliComplete
www.flashpeak.com

AlphaSmart – manufacturer of Dana portable computer
Northway House, 1379 High Road, Whetstone, London, N20 9LP
Tel: 020 8492 3690
Email: UK-info@alphasmart.com
Website: www.alphasmart.co.uk

TAG Learning – recommended supplier of AlphaSmart Dana
25 Pelham Road, Gravesend, Kent, DA11 0HU
Tel: 01474 357350
Email: sales@taglearning.com
Website: www.taglearning.com

StoryCraft Pro
www.storycraftpro.com

StoryWeaver
www.storymind.com

WriteItNow
www.ravensheadservices.com

Final Draft
www.finaldraft.com
Price (Amazon.co.uk): £169.14

Chapter 16

A selection of writing courses available in the UK:

Liberato
9 Bishops Avenue, Bishops Stortford, Hertfordshire, CM23 3EJ
Tel: 01279 833690
Email: liberato@tesco.net
Website: www.liberato.co.uk

The Writers Bureau
Sevendale House, 7 Dale Street, Manchester, M1 1JB
Tel: 0800 856 2008
Email: studentservices@writersbureau.com
Website: www.writersbureau.com

The Writing College
16 Magdalen Road, Exeter, EX2 4SY
Tel: 0800 328 9396
Email: enquiries@writingcollege.com
Website: www.writingcollege.com

Writers' News Home Study Division
1st Floor, Victoria House, 143-145 The Headrow, Leeds, LS1 5RL
Tel: 0113 200 2917
Email: rachel.bellerby@writersnews.co.uk
Website: www.writersnews.co.uk

Writingclasses.co.uk
Tel: 0131 554 1857
Email: marianne@writingclasses.co.uk
Website: www.writingclasses.co.uk

National Extension College
The Michael Young Centre, Purbeck Road, Cambridge, CB2 2HN
Tel: 0800 389 2839
Email: courses@nec.ac.uk
Website: www.nec.ac.uk

Chapter 18

Editorial, advisory and critique services:

Jacqui Bennett Writer's Bureau
87 Home Orchard, Yate, South Gloucestershire, BS37 5XH
Tel: 01454 324717
Email: jenny@jbwb.co.uk
Website: www.jbwb.co.uk

The Hilary Johnson Authors' Advisory Service
1 Beechwood Court, Syderstone, Norfolk, PE31 8TR
Tel: 01485 578594
Email: hilary@hilaryjohnson.demon.co.uk
Website: www.hilaryjohnson.demon.co.uk

The Literary Consultancy
Diorama Arts, 34 Osnaburgh Street, London, NW1 3ND
Tel: 020 7813 4330
Email: info@literaryconsultancy.co.uk
Website: www.literaryconsultancy.co.uk

Chapter 19

The Society of Authors
84 Drayton Gardens, London, SW10 9SB
Tel: 020 7373 6642
Email: use enquiry form on website
Website: www.societyofauthors.net

Audacity – free audio editing software
Website: audacity.sourceforge.net

The Writers' and Artist's Yearbook 2005
ISBN: 0713669365
Publisher: A & C Black (2004)
Price (Amazon.co.uk): £9.79

The Writer's Handbook 2005
ISBN: 1405041536
Publisher: Macmillan (2004)
Price (Amazon.co.uk): £8.39

Publishing News
7 John Street, London, WC1N 2ES
Tel: 0870 870 2345
Email: rodneyburbeck@publishingnews.co.uk
Website: www.publishingnews.co.uk

The Bookseller
5th Floor, Endeavour House, 189 Shaftesbury Avenue, London,
WC2H 8TJ
Tel: 020 7420 6006
Website: www.thebookseller.com

Association of Authors' Agents
www.agentsassoc.co.uk

Everyone Who's Anyone
UK, US & Canadian Publishers, Editors and Agents
www.everyonewhosanyone.com

Book Trust
45 East Hill, London, SW18 2QZ
Tel: 020 8516 2977
Email: info@booktrust.org.uk
Website: www.booktrust.org.uk

1001 Ways to Market Your Books
by John Kremer
ISBN: 0912411481
Publisher: Open Horizons Publishing Company (2000)
Price (Amazon.co.uk): £13.09

Appendix B   200 What Ifs

Playing 'what if' is a great way of generating ideas. Have a look through these and apply a little lateral thinking to see what you can come up with:

Animals
- What if cows were carnivores?
- What if fish swam in the air as well as in water?
- What if cats had eight legs and could do everything that spiders can do?
- What if your pet caused an accident?

At home
- What if your furniture had emotions?
- What if you woke up in someone else's body?
- What if you found buried treasure in your garden?
- What if you were at war with your neighbours?
- What if your child was more intelligent than you?
- What if you thought that you were an orphan but then your parents turned up?
- What if someone wanted to buy your children?
- What if a man claiming to be your long-lost brother turned up at your house?
- What if you were under house arrest?
- What if you woke up crying or screaming but you didn't know why?
- What if someone was hiding under your bed?
- What if you went to visit your family but the entire street had been demolished and you didn't know where they were?
- What if you had to flee your home?
- What if you gave up trying to be a success yourself and concentrated on making your children successful?

- What if your child wanted to follow in your footsteps but you didn't want them to?
- What if your child's teacher took you aside for a quiet word?

At work

- What if you told a joke to someone without a sense of humour?
- What if you were inundated with complaints about something you had done?
- What if you received too many orders?
- What if you were given a job that you knew nothing about?
- What if you offered a service that had never been offered before?
- What if your boss disappeared and was never seen again?
- What if you were put in charge of an inquiry but suspected that you might get into trouble if you revealed the truth?
- What if your company's team-building weekend turned into something very different?
- What if you turned up for work one day and found yourself already sitting at your desk?
- What if you were forced to accept a pay cut?
- What if something important happened at work when you weren't there?
- What if the new boss was turning a great company into a bad one?
- What if you were summoned to the manager's office?
- What if your job evolved into something completely different?
- What if you had two jobs that conflicted with each other?
- What if you stole your employer's customer database and used it to set up your own company?
- What if you clinched the deal at the very last moment?
- What if your biggest customer was on the verge of walking out?
- What if a rival company started up and was undercutting your prices?
- What if you were in charge of poaching customers from a rival company?

- What if your boss told you that you were being posted abroad?
- What if your boss stopped you from going on a course that would benefit your career?
- What if you embarrassed your boss?

Crime

- What if someone was arrested for murdering you?
- What if you were in jail?
- What if you committed an offence without realising that you had done so?
- What if you found a dead body at the back of your wardrobe?
- What if you solved a crime that had been unsolved for years?
- What if you were harbouring a fugitive?
- What if your getaway car was stolen while you were robbing a bank?
- What if someone was attacked while they were speaking to you on the phone?
- What if the Queen personally made all laws?
- What if there was a national break-a-law day?
- What if the police advised you to change your phone number?
- What if you were stopped by the police?
- What if you had the same surname as a notorious criminal and people assumed that you were from the same family?
- What if everyone was a criminal?

Dedication

- What if you learnt a new skill?
- What if you were dedicated to your cause?
- What if you threw out the rule book and did things your way?

Desperate measures

- What if it was up to you to keep things going?
- What if everyone was depending on you?
- What if you turned to violence as a last resort?

- What if you'd tried everything else, so this was your final attempt?
- What if a tactic or trick you'd always relied upon didn't work?
- What if every time someone did you wrong you made a note of it and got your revenge exactly one year later?
- What if you were awarded a medal for bravery?
- What if you deliberately gave someone a gift that you knew they'd hate?
- What if you decided to cheat?
- What if you decided to stop being nice to people and be ruthless instead?
- What if the only way to survive was to severely injure yourself?
- What if you did something controversial?
- What if you were surrounded?
- What if you were engulfed in flames?
- What if you would die before help arrived?
- What if the bomb would explode before you could get to it?
- What if you had to escape from a burning building?
- What if you decided to put up a fight?
- What if the door locked behind you and you didn't have a key?
- What if you received an urgent phone call?
- What if things had gone far enough and you wouldn't stand for it anymore?
- What if you had a sense of impending doom?

Health
- What if you were allergic to water?
- What if you were allergic to the opposite sex?
- What if your life was changed by an 'extreme makeover'?
- What if you were in hospital but you didn't know why?
- What if your attempts at self-help went badly wrong?
- What if you pretended that you were seriously ill to get people to donate money to you?
- What if a drug you bought on the internet had an unexpected effect?
- What if you couldn't get clean?

- What if you were saved by your guardian angel?
- What if you needed surgery?
- What if you needed to go abroad for treatment?
- What if your doctor got your medical records muddled up with somebody else's?
- What if you suffered an injury while in hospital?
- What if you planned your own funeral?

History

- What if past-life regression revealed that you had never lived before?
- What if you came across an ancient statue that looked exactly like you?
- What if you found a portrait of yourself hanging in the Louvre?

Money

- What if you gambled your life savings on a horse?
- What if you invested all your money in a company that went bust?
- What if your bank manager changed his mind?
- What if your children found your secret 'rainy day' fund and spent it all?
- What if transferring money out of the country was prohibited?
- What if every community had its own currency?
- What if the only way to get the thing you wanted was to win it?
- What if entry was free but you had to pay to get out - but you didn't know that?
- What if you paid in a very large cheque at your bank, but the money never made it into your account?
- What if a price was wrongly marked?
- What if a special offer wasn't quite what it seemed?
- What if you got more than you bargained for?
- What if you needed to cut expenditure severely?
- What if you were sold something by someone who didn't know what they were selling?

- What if you felt that you deserved a much bigger reward than you actually received?
- What if your accountant got his sums badly wrong?
- What if you couldn't buy anything, only rent it?
- What if you did everything for money?

Other people

- What if an offer of help was withdrawn?
- What if a request for help was refused?
- What if someone tried to deny you a proper education?
- What if you were afraid of people called John (or some other name)?
- What if someone admired your body but you'd prefer it if they admired your brain (or vice versa)?
- What if an artist wanted to paint your portrait?
- What if you were mistaken for someone else?
- What if your neighbours were spying on you?

Oops!

- What if your spelling mistakes got you into trouble?
- What if you did all the right things but in the wrong order?
- What if you broke a mirror?
- What if you scratched an itch at precisely the wrong moment?
- What if you were invited onto a TV show but got into a row with one of the other guests?
- What if you received a gift that you didn't want?
- What if you were unsure of the rules?
- What if it was supposed to be a nice surprise but it all went terribly wrong?
- What if someone overestimated or underestimated your intelligence or ability?
- What if curiosity got the better of you?
- What if you weren't where you were supposed to be?
- What if nobody was prepared to join your campaign?
- What if you walked in your sleep – and did other things too?
- What if you forgot something important?
- What if your chimney caught fire?
- What if your application was turned down?

- What if someone made you an amazing offer but left before they put it in writing?
- What if you attracted a crowd?
- What if you forgot to check your facts?
- What if you suddenly realised that you needed a lot more practise?
- What if you gave someone some advice that they didn't want?
- What if you had a moment of enlightenment?
- What if you weren't sure?
- What if you were deceived by appearances?
- What if you had too much of a good thing?
- What if a woman you admired turned out to be a man?
- What if you came to the wrong conclusion?
- What if you fell asleep at an inappropriate time?
- What if you held out for a better offer but it never came?
- What if you made a promise that you were unable to keep?
- What if everything happened much sooner than you expected?

Science fiction

- What if time passed more slowly in some parts of the world?
- What if you were genetically modified?
- What if you could see radio waves?
- What if the pattern of day (light) and night (dark) was not regular?
- What if light ebbed and flowed like the tide and was affected by the Moon?
- What if there was no oxygen twenty feet above sea level?
- What if the higher up you went, the lighter (or heavier) you became?
- What if something impossible happened every day?
- What if you could take a pill that would make you dream?
- What if the atomic bomb had been developed in ancient times?
- What if you were visible to women but invisible to men (or vice versa if you prefer)?

Technology

- What if your computer was more intelligent than you?
- What if you misunderstood the instructions?
- What if one of the keys on your keyboard didn't work so you never used that letter?
- What if your computer wouldn't let you turn it off?
- What if you found a strange file on your computer?
- What if you couldn't do anything without an instruction manual?

Travel

- What if you were stopped by customs officers?
- What if you were arrested when you tried to bring back a souvenir from your holiday?
- What if you made a wrong turn?
- What if the traffic lights remained on red?

Miscellaneous

- What if you tried to get on TV?
- What if you were accused of being old-fashioned?
- What if you had a very common name?
- What if you were ahead of your time?
- What if you were addicted to something unusual?
- What if all your birthdays came at once?
- What if you looked in a mirror and saw something that wasn't really there?
- What if you read an announcement in the newspaper that you were to be married – which was the first you'd heard of it?
- What if you gave up watching the news or reading newspapers because you'd rather not know what was happening?
- What if you received an anonymous letter?
- What if you became a catwalk model?
- What if library membership was compulsory?
- What if you spent a day saying 'yes' instead of 'no' and 'no' instead of 'yes'?
- What if you went to a fancy dress party and nobody knew who you really were?

- What if you refused to go along with everyone else?
- What if you began to change?
- What if a new episode of a TV show was being broadcast for the first time, but you were convinced that you'd seen it before?
- What if you rehearsed everything you said and did?
- What if you decided to sell out?
- What if you were afraid of mirrors?
- What if you had an ambition that could never be achieved?
- What if you dared someone to do something that ended up severely injuring them?
- What if you were invited to a party by someone you didn't know?

There are hundreds more What Ifs in the members' Archive at ideas4writers.co.uk

ideas4writers.co.uk

The ideas and inspiration website for all writers

Three months free membership

To claim your free ideas4writers.co.uk membership, complete the details below, then detach this page* and send it to:

ideas4writers
PO Box 49
Cullompton
Devon
EX15 1WX

Please write clearly – if we can't read it we won't be able to process your membership.

_____

Full name:

Email address**:

Password:
(choose a password between 6 and 12 characters long)

Telephone number:
(in case we can't contact you by email)

Tick here if you're already a member ☐
(we'll extend your current membership by 3 months)

ideas4writers will not pass your details on to anyone else

* No photocopies accepted
** Email address and internet access required

0955011604/FWWB0505